Teachers' working conditions are the flip side of students' learning conditions. We have a high-school dropout problem in large part because we have a teacher dropout problem. If, as Eklund suggests, we listen to teachers and make sure schools are satisfying places for them to work, our students will be the greatest beneficiaries.

Ken Futernick, Ph.D., Professor of Education and Director of K–12 Studies at the Center for Teacher Quality, California State University, Sacramento

This book is a lifeline for every administrator, teacher, and parent who understands that if schools are to be great places for children, then our classrooms need to be staffed by intelligent, passionate, and caring teachers. Eklund maps out guiding principles and a systematic approach for cultivating a workplace that works for teachers.

Sam Intrator, Professor, Smith College and coeditor of Teaching with Fire: Poetry That Sustains the Courage to Teach

Schools could be much more effective with kids if the adults trusted and valued each other at high levels. Having hard conversations together is the best place for us to go. With those conversations gradually comes a sense of worth and collaboration. I sincerely believe in the message of this book.

Mary Beth Blegen, National Teacher of the Year, 1996

Search Institute's 40 Developmental Assets are as applicable and meaningful for adults as they are for youth. *How Was Your Day at School?* provides a realistic, insightful look at our lives as educators and demonstrates how asset building nurtures, motivates, and sustains us personally and professionally throughout our careers.

Rusty Clifford, Ph.D., Superintendent of West Carrollton Schools, West Carrollton, Ohio

D0840178

How Was *Your* Day at School?

Improving Dialogue about Teacher Job Satisfaction

NATHAN EKLUND, M.ED.

SEARCH
INSTITUTE
PRESS

How Was *Your* Day at School?
Improving Dialogue about Teacher
Job Satisfaction
Nathan Eklund, M. Ed.

The following are registered trademarks
of Search Institute: Search Institute®,
Developmental Assets®, and

Search Institute Press
Minneapolis, Minnesota
Copyright © 2008 by Search Institute

All rights reserved. No parts of this
publication may be reproduced in any
manner, mechanical or electronic,
without prior permission from the
publisher except in brief quotations or
summaries in articles or reviews, or as
individual activity sheets for educational
non-commercial use only. For additional
permission, visit Search Institute's
Web site at www.search-institute.org/
permissions and submit a Permissions
Request Form.

At the time of publication, all facts
and figures cited herein are the
most current available; all telephone
numbers, addresses, and Web site
URLs are accurate and active; all
publications, organizations, Web sites,
and other resources exist as described
in this book; and all efforts have been
made to verify them. The author and
Search Institute make no warranty or
guarantee concerning the information
and materials given out by organizations
or content found at Web sites that are
cited herein, and we are not responsible
for any changes that occur after this
book's publication. If you find an error
or believe that a resource listed herein
is not as described, please contact Client
Services at Search Institute.

10 9 8 7 6 5 4 3 2 1

Printed on acid-free paper in the United
States of America.

Search Institute
615 First Avenue Northeast, Suite 125
Minneapolis, MN 55413
www.search-institute.org
612-376-8955 • 800-888-7828

ISBN-13: 978-1-57482-264-9

Credits
Editor: Tenessa Gemelke
Copyeditor: Kate Brielmaier
Book Design: Jeenee Lee
Production Supervisor:
  Mary Ellen Buscher

**Library of Congress
Cataloging-in-Publication Data**
Eklund, Nathan.
    How was your day at school? :
improving dialogue about teacher job
satisfaction / Nathan Eklund.
    p. cm.
Includes index.
ISBN 978-1-57482-264-9
(pbk. : alk. paper)
1. Teachers--Job stress--United States.
2. Teacher turnover--United States.
3. Burn out (Psychology)
4. Teachers--Psychology. I. Title.
LB2840.2.E39 2008
371.1001'9--dc22
                    2008029757

About This Resource
The research for this book was funded
in part by a grant from the Curtis L.
Carlson Family Foundation. Search
Institute and the author are grateful for
this support.

Licensing and Copyright
The handouts from *How Was* Your *Day
at School? Improving Dialogue about
Teacher Job Satisfaction* on the CD-ROM
may be copied as needed for educational,
noncommercial use. Please see the list
of CD-ROM handouts at the front of this
book for further guidelines.

Contents

List of CD-ROM Handouts

You may find some of the content in this book useful as you facilitate discussions or plan efforts with colleagues. To make it easier for you to distribute this information, we have redesigned many of the concepts in the form of reproducible handouts. The titles below are the abbreviated file names that you will find on the CD-ROM.

Licensing and Copyright

The CD-ROM handouts from *How Was Your Day at School? Improving Dialogue about Teacher Job Satisfaction* may be copied as needed for educational, noncommercial use. For each copy, please respect the following guidelines:

- Do not remove, alter, or obscure the Search Institute credit and copyright information on any activity sheet.

- Clearly differentiate any material you add for local distribution from material prepared by Search Institute.

- Do not alter the Search Institute material in content or meaning.

- Do not resell the activity sheets for profit.

- Include the following attribution when you use the information from the handouts in other formats for promotional or educational purposes: **Reprinted with permission from *How Was Your Day at School? Improving Dialogue about Teacher Job Satisfaction* (specify the title of the handout you are quoting). Copyright © 2008 Search Institute®, Minneapolis, MN; 800-888-7828; www.search-institute.org. All rights reserved.**

Foreword:
Hope for Teachers

This book found me at just the right time in my teaching career. I was three years into a second career, teaching about language arts and life to middle school students. In my earlier days of teaching, I had been full of energy, enthusiasm and ideas. I recall saying to several friends and family members that I couldn't believe they were paying me to do this work that I loved. But a tough year of stress and student issues and both minor and major obstacles had led me to be burnt out, frustrated and lacking in the will to go on. I thought to myself, "Is it supposed to be this hard?" "Should I really feel this bad when a day is done?" "Do I want to continue in a profession that I love, but that ultimately is taking a toll on my health and my happiness?"

And I wasn't alone. All around me, colleagues both new and experienced were feeling the same frustration and futility that I was. I would sit at my desk at the end of a long and challenging day and wonder what in the world I was going to do next.

And then my close friend Tenessa Gemelke told me how excited she was about this book she was editing at Search Institute. She knew I was struggling with my own job satisfaction, and she asked me to review an early version of the author's manuscript. I said I'd be happy to read it, but I was secretly rolling my eyes. I figured she was just introducing me to another person who had some magic cure for teachers to feel better and produce more, adding one more thing to their overflowing plates.

But I was wrong. This book is not just a pat on the head to hardworking professionals. This book has real ideas, real tools to help educators make changes. As I read, I began to feel that old energy, that enthusiasm creep into me. I was making notes, using the personal inventories, dreaming big dreams for myself and for my students.

The message that truly resonates with me is Mr. Eklund's assertion that what is good for the *teachers* is good for the *students*. And I am proof of that. Reading the book gave me a sense of purpose and a belief that the change that I want to see can start with me. Even when there are roadblocks, there are always ways around them if I am willing to reflect, rethink, and persevere. This optimism has given me renewed energy for my students.

I encourage anyone who cares about children and the future of education to read this book. If you are a teacher, an administrator, a parent or a community member, this book can help you see how you can play a role in bettering our educational system toward the happiness and health of our children.

As for me, I am starting with myself. Every day now I take time to ask myself, "How was your day at school?" I will use the insights and tools from this book again and again. I hope it gives you the same new passion and energy for your profession that it has given me.

Carla Smith is a 7th grade Language Arts teacher in Moorhead, Minnesota. She holds a Bachelors degree in University Studies (English and Mass Communications) from Moorhead State University and a Masters in Education from the University of St. Thomas.

Foreword:
Help for Administrators

The 40 Developmental Assets framework is the most powerful tool for educators that I've encountered in my 20 years as a classroom teacher, high school counselor, and middle school administrator. When I started using this approach, it totally changed the conversations I was having with students and parents. It broadened my perspective.

By focusing on strengths and opportunities, I helped students identify supportive relationships in their lives and started using those relationships to inspire more success.

Several months ago, after a Developmental Assets training, a group of teachers approached me and asked the question, "How can we build assets in kids if we don't have them ourselves?" This question reflects the tremendous stress that teachers experience every day. Teachers report that they are being asked to do more and more without being given additional resources. They feel isolated from other adults in the building. They often spend extra hours after school or in the evening to prepare for the next day.

We provide teachers with many professional development opportunities, but schools do too little to address the personal stressors that impact teachers daily. My staff's question was evidence that we needed to help teachers experience assets for themselves. I turned to Search Institute for help and was excited to hear that Nathan Eklund was already working on the topic. Another administrator and I spent a day with him just as he was finishing this book. We discussed ways that schools can build assets for the *adults* in the building, not just the students. As we headed back to the airport that day, I saw new dimensions to the asset framework and realized that it's *imperative* that we do this work.

Applying an asset-focused approach to the adults in your building is a lot like applying it to young people: it's "common sense" but not always "common practice." This book has inspired immediate changes in the way I work and talk with staff. I now realize that schools tend to focus on professional development to the neglect of personal development. Now, when teachers e-mail me with concerns, I intentionally make the effort to seek them out and talk about the concern face-to-face. I take more time to talk with teachers about their lives outside of school, recognizing that their lives impact who they are in the classroom. Our staff wellness team has created adult asset-building opportunities that mirror the work we do with our students. When teachers feel the power of supportive coworkers or see their ideas implemented in the building, they are much better at creating similarly positive experiences for their students.

We know that students with more assets are more likely to thrive and are less vulnerable to risk behaviors. The same can be said for our teachers. Teachers with more assets are better able to cope with all the demands placed on them and less vulnerable to burnout. In the end, asset-rich teachers are better teachers.

There is no question that teachers have a lot on their plates. As administrators, we may not always be able to remove items from a teacher's plate, but we can sure work to make the plate stronger. By changing the conversations and interactions you have with the adults in your school, this book will help you do just that. I challenge you to turn these common sense ideas into common practice in your building. You'll see results.

Scott Butler is Assistant Principal at Beadle Elementary School in Millard, Nebraska.

Preface:
Why I Left (and Didn't Leave) Teaching

I taught high school English for twelve wonderful years. As with all teachers, it's not enough to say that I "taught" and leave it at that. I also coached soccer, directed theater productions, managed the literary arts magazine, acted as department head, and generally involved myself in the life of the school as much as I could without losing my mind. I loved my students and colleagues. I felt embraced by the community. I came into the district as a single college graduate and left as a married father of two. My teaching was entirely the setting for my own transformation into an adult.

And then I left. I left while I still loved teaching. At the time of my departure, my students were still paramount in my life. I was still learning, still developing new classes, and still excited about teaching in general. My colleagues were and remain some of the best friends I have in this world.

So why did I leave a profession that meant so much to me? During my last years in the classroom, I had become increasingly concerned about the state of teacher burnout and job attrition. As a department head, I worked with colleagues to resolve conflicts, establish shared goals, and create a work culture that allowed for healthy and balanced expectations. Our department successfully overcame a variety of obstacles, but I remained frustrated when I saw promising but unhappy educators working long, difficult hours on a path toward burnout. I also knew that I never wanted to become one of those unhappy teachers. If I was ever going to leave teaching, I was going to do so while I was still engaged and enthused.

The more I thought about these issues, the more I realized that I had work to do outside of the classroom. Just as I had felt called to teaching in the first place, I now felt compelled to find a new role for myself as an educator.

So before the first day of soccer started in late summer, I decided that I was going to coach and teach for one more year. I told only a few of my closest friends. I was going to spend my last year fully relishing all aspects of teaching, even the things I didn't ordinarily enjoy. I gave myself one year to soak up every minute with my students and fellow teachers. The whole year was surreal and amazingly fulfilling. I couldn't believe that I wasn't going to be a teacher anymore.

At this point I still didn't have a definite plan about what I would do next. As I pondered my wide-open future, I realized that there were questions I needed to ask: "What do I want to do? Whom do I want to help? What fulfills me?" It was this questioning that brought me to the realization that it was the teachers who beckoned to me. In a sense, I was ready to leave the classroom, but I wasn't ready to leave the profession of teaching. But now the question was, how could I best channel this desire to work on behalf of educators? Run for office? Become an administrator? Somewhere there had to be an answer.

As I faced these questions, Search Institute's framework of Developmental Assets® seeped into my thinking. I had been familiar with the research for years, but now I sat down to read *Great Places to Learn* by Neal Starkman, Peter Scales, and Clay Roberts. Their vision of a school where students and adults were engaged with one another in strength-based relationships resonated with me very powerfully. There was something in the assets that held a key—not only for me, but also for the educators I wanted to serve. Here I encountered some of the same questions I had been exploring during my last year of teaching.

My epiphany occurred on page 17 of *Great Places to Learn*. The chapter is titled "Why We Should Build Assets in School Communities." Here are the sentences that inspired the book you're reading now:

- Haven't you accomplished more when you felt good about coming to work?

- Aren't you spurred on to do greater things when you know that your colleagues will respect and be receptive to your ideas?

- Don't you feel more capable when everything and everyone around you supports who you are and what you do?[1]

The authors had introduced these questions in the context of building assets for students, but it occurred to me that we rarely stop to consider the ramifications of these questions for ourselves as educators.

These questions succinctly capture the conditions in which educators (and all workers) can be happy, healthy, and successful. I knew that whatever I did next, I wanted to work on these possibilities. I wanted to help teachers and administrators believe that feeling good about the work they do is not just a nice idea, but also *an achievable reality*. I wanted to strive toward the day when all educators in all schools could answer these questions with a resounding "YES!" and confirm that this is truly the kind of workplace they experience every day.

Fortunately Search Institute was ready to embark on this challenge with me, and this book is our first effort to document the exciting discoveries we're making as we conduct trainings and do consulting work with schools that are striving to improve teacher job satisfaction. I hope the pages that follow fill you with the same optimism and encouragement I feel toward the future of teaching.

Notes

1. Starkman, N., Scales, P. C., & Roberts, C. (1999, 2006). *Great places to learn: Creating asset-building schools that help students succeed,* 2d ed. Minneapolis, MN: Search Institute.

Introduction:
How Was Your Day at School?

Read that question again. What do you picture? Where does the scene take place? Who is there? What's the response?

If you're like me, your first instinct is to picture a parent, perhaps in a kitchen, talking to a student getting home from school. In fact, I ask my own son that same question every day when he arrives home from elementary school. The response is usually something unenthusiastic like "fine" or "okay." I try daily to press him for a more significant answer, but I'm continually met with the typical grunted response.

In truth, this is actually a powerful question. When we ask this of our children, we want to know: What did you learn today? Were people nice to you? Did you succeed at something? Are you happy? Do you like school? Are you okay? These are not trivial concerns. We ask with the deepest consideration and compassion. The grunted answer may be neither sufficient nor very encouraging, but we still recognize how important it is to investigate the well-being of children. In fact, researcher Peter Scales highlights the significance of this question:

> All the dropout prevention and school reform literature can be reduced to a single conclusion: Young people are more likely to stay in school and do well there (or any other program) if they like it there. And they are more likely to like schools if they feel safe there, if they have successes there, if their friends, neighbors, and family are proud of what they do there, if they

have fun there, and if they feel someone in the school cares for them.[1]

So let me direct this question to you. Maybe you're a first-year teacher, looking for guidance as you fulfill your lifelong desire to work in a classroom. Maybe you're a seasoned administrator, struggling against the statistics that show teachers leaving the profession at alarming rates. Regardless of your role in education, don't you deserve the same consideration as your students? How was *your* day at school? Did anyone ask you this question today? If so, did you answer with a one-word grunt?

Now ask yourself again, and consider the ramifications this simple question raises. In order to answer it with any degree of accuracy, we have to ponder a host of related questions:

How did your students behave today?

How did your plans go?

How did you sleep last night?

How many minutes did you get to yourself today?

How are you feeling about your work?

What excited you today?

How safe did you feel at work?

How were your colleagues?

How many meetings did you have?

How much grading do you have to do?

When's the last time you exercised or took time for yourself?

The challenges involved in a single day of teaching are staggering— and therein lie the joys, struggles, rewards, sacrifices, benefits, and reality of being an educator.

As you reflect on what it means to be committed to sustaining yourself and others in the work of education, remember to stop and ask yourself this question with all the care and consideration you would give a student. Use this book as an opportunity to engage in an intentional, thoughtful inquiry that will lead you to your own answers about improving job satisfaction for yourself and your coworkers.

Defining the Challenge

I began researching this book with a simple premise in mind: Teacher job satisfaction *matters*. Obviously it mattered to me, having been a teacher for twelve years, but I thought the larger relevance was perfectly clear until I sought to get funding for the research in this book. Initial financial support came from the Curtis L. Carlson Family Foundation; before they signed off on the project, they challenged me to consider the following query:

> We *fund projects that help students succeed.*
> *How does helping teachers help students?*

At first I was flabbergasted by the question. I had taken it for granted that a positive work climate for teachers was central to student success. When I stopped to think about it, though, I realized that we nearly always frame education issues in terms of the student, not the educator. For example, when we read news reports about class size, we focus entirely on the effect class size has on student achievement and behavior. We pay little or no attention to the effect class size has on the educator. The difference between spending an hour teaching 25 students versus teaching 35 or more may seem insignificant to the average person, but teachers know the dramatic effect of such an increase.

A colleague once told me that for every student above 30 in a classroom, it feels like teaching 10 more. I heard this in the halcyon days when I still had only 17 students in my classes. It wasn't until my classes grew to 30, then 32, then 36 and above that I truly understood what my colleague meant. My response, like that of all dedicated teachers, was to try to teach better or harder to lessen the negative effects that increased class sizes had on our students.

Here's the question I've posed as I continue my research: Don't large class sizes harm students *because* they cause teachers increased fatigue and decreased job satisfaction? In this case, isn't diminished learning for students inextricably linked to educators' increased workloads and decreased morale? Yet this is not the angle mass media or the general public takes toward trends such as these. Not only does public discourse fail to recognize the relevance of the toll on educators, but it also seems to increase public scrutiny and criticism of teachers.

Once I made this connection, I became convinced that creating a positive school climate for teachers is not a side issue to or a distraction from student success, but actually a central solution to so many of the obstacles we work to overcome. The truth is this:

- When I was happier and more relaxed as a teacher, I was able to work harder for others.

- When I was happier and more relaxed as a teacher, I was a better colleague.

- When I was happier and more relaxed as a teacher, my students performed better.

The multiple benefits of my increased professional happiness were so powerful in my experience that I began to see the relevance throughout the field of education.

The opposite side of the coin, of course, is what happens when teachers are unhappy and facing excessive stress. I'm certain that during the periods when I was not as satisfied or joyful in my work, my students suffered. I can confirm this with a quick review of my own mental list of unsatisfying circumstances:

- Fatigue from the repetition of teaching the same content every year

- Conflicts with administration

- Distance from or discord with colleagues

- Personal fatigue, especially as it affected my family

- Lack of decision-making power or control

- Too many roles to play as an educator

In my own work life and in the experiences of my colleagues, I saw how such challenges drain a teacher's energy. These obstacles rob us of concentration and enthusiasm. They can make us tired, discouraged, and cynical. The net result is not simply unhappiness or frustration, but a dramatic decrease in our ability to focus on our students.

As I argued my case and laid the groundwork for this research, I restated my initial premise: Teacher job satisfaction matters not only to teachers, *but also to students*. This work is not about increasing teacher morale alone. It is about increasing staff and individual morale because students benefit from relaxed, happy, fulfilled, and engaged teachers.

The Realities of Teacher Burnout

When pressed to think solely about themselves, apart from the students, educators are often reluctant, insisting, "We can't think about ourselves. We don't have time. What about the kids?" In fact, even the concept of thinking about the *students* might appear luxurious in today's educational arena. Mandated testing and performance benchmarks are tied to instruction, creating an environment in which one "teaches to the test." This can make us feel detached from the students, to say nothing of our colleagues or ourselves. Unfortunately, the research on teacher burnout reveals that a failure to focus on the needs of teachers has grim consequences.

What follows is a three-pronged definition of burnout. As you read these descriptions, consider how each experience erodes the job satisfaction of educators:

> ***Emotional Exhaustion*** Teachers feel that they can no longer give of themselves to students as they did earlier in their careers.

> ***Depersonalization*** Teachers develop negative, cynical, and sometimes callous attitudes toward students, parents, and/or colleagues.

> ***Diminished Personal Accomplishment*** Teachers perceive themselves as ineffective in helping students learn, and unmotivated in fulfilling their other school responsibilities.[2]

These traits reflect the factors that dictate whether or not you have a good day at work. Just as bad days are marked by the descriptions above, good days are marked by enough energy to give to others, positive views of your work, colleagues, and students, and the intrinsic feeling of knowing that you are good at what you do.

As you look at your own workplace, it may be difficult to see the connections between this research and your daily experience of being a teacher. Think about these questions:

- What makes a good day at work for you?

- What makes a bad day?

- What saves a bad day for you?

These questions are about what really matters to you. If your bad day was about your lessons not going well, or conflicts with other adults, what does that say about how you connect to your work? If a good day was about feeling like you were reaching students or having a positive effect on colleagues, what does this reflect about your values and the elements that keep you from burning out?

Many of these burnout traits end up being a product of how we experience positive relationships with others: Are we told when we've done a good job? Do we have others to cheer for us and pick us up during difficult times? Do we have others helping us discover options for personal health and success? This book helps you recognize the factors in your work that draw you toward happiness and support and away from burning out.

In many ways, burnout is something you can gauge on your way home from school every day. Picture a horrible day at work. Go straight from your classroom to your car and drive home. How do you feel once you get home? How do you feel going back the next day? Now imagine the same bad day, but before you leave, you are able to connect with a colleague to discuss the day, vent, and think about tomorrow. Now drive home. How different is that experience?

Freudenberger, a researcher who coined the term "burnout" in the 1970s, describes the condition as a "state of exhaustion that resulted from working too intensely and without concern for one's own needs."[3] He found that burnout described those who paid a high price for what he saw as an overzealous desire to help others.

If Freudenberger is correct, then educators must reassess what it means to work on behalf of students. In many educational settings, there are teachers who embrace misery as a normal part of the job. In other words: "If I can be (or appear) more miserable than my coworkers, then I'm somehow teaching better." This mindset uses exhaustion, tension, nervousness, and perhaps even sadness as higher marks of honor than peace, energy, and a heightened sense of purpose in our teaching.

At the end of the day, think of the tremendous loss to an educational system that does little to address burnout among staff. It is a lose-lose proposition. The teachers are wiped out and discouraged, and it's difficult to imagine that the students are benefiting under these circumstances. Following this line of reasoning, then, educators may want to rethink the generally held mantra of "it's all about the kids."

What's Good for the Teachers Is Good for the Students

Few people would argue with the notion that if we do not take care of ourselves, we are unable to take care of others. As we work to improve the dialogue around teacher morale and work climate, it is helpful to stop and make additional comparisons between healthy educators and healthy students.

Search Institute, a nonprofit research organization focusing on positive youth development, has identified a framework of 40 Developmental Assets; this framework describes the positive qualities, experiences, and opportunities that all young people need in their lives. (For a complete list of assets for youth, see pages 153–155.) Research links these healthy traits to positive behaviors and outcomes, and the absence of assets is likewise linked to unhealthy behaviors and negative outcomes for young people.

The Developmental Assets are firmly grounded in research and common sense. The structure of these assets comes through eight asset categories, or eight basic areas of positive human development. The first four categories comprise the *external* assets that youth need developed around them. Four additional categories spell out the *internal* assets that youth need to develop as they mature. There is a brief description of the asset categories on the following page.

 [*See handout* **INTRO 1** *on CD-ROM*]

ASSET CATEGORIES

External Assets (the external structures, relationships, and activities that create a positive environment):

Support • Young people need to be surrounded by people who love, care for, appreciate, and accept them. They need to know that they belong and that they are not alone.

Empowerment • Young people need to feel valued and valuable. They need to feel safe, to believe that they are liked and respected, and to have opportunities to make meaningful contributions within the hierarchies that surround them.

Boundaries and Expectations • Young people need the positive influence of peers and adults who encourage them to be and do their best. They need clear rules about appropriate behavior, and consistent, reasonable consequences for inappropriate behaviors.

Constructive Use of Time • Young people need opportunities—outside of school—to learn and develop new skills and interests, and to spend enjoyable time interacting with other youth and adults.

Internal Assets (the values, skills, and beliefs necessary to fully engage with other people and function well in the world):

Commitment to Learning • Young people need a variety of learning experiences, including the desire for academic success, a sense of the lasting importance of learning, and a belief in their own abilities.

Positive Values • Young people need to develop strong guiding values or principles, including caring for others, having high standards for personal character, and believing in protecting their own well-being.

Social Competencies • Young people need to develop the skills to interact effectively with others, to make difficult decisions and choices, and to cope with new situations.

Positive Identity • Young people need to believe in their own self-worth, to feel that they have control over the things that happen to them, and to have a sense of purpose in life as well as a positive view of the future.

As you read through these simple but powerful concepts, pause for a moment. Go back and read through each category again. Only this time, when you read the words "young people," replace that phrase with "educators." The resonance of these asset categories with our own experience is striking. Although Search Institute's research has focused on children and teenagers, we can see that these internal and external opportunities are things that all people, regardless of age, need in order to be healthy and happy.

At the core of this thinking is the notion that if something's good for the kids, it's good for the adults. In fact, teachers who have been working with this framework in schools do indeed report that they enjoy their jobs more and feel better about their teaching. The obvious progression of this notion has led these teachers to ask the question, "How can we build assets for our students if we don't experience them ourselves?"

If educators focus exclusively on building strengths in students, the effect on their own job satisfaction and professional development is oftentimes secondary and haphazard. But what might happen if we apply the same strength-based, positive development model *intentionally* and *consistently* in the lives of educators? What if the systems in which teachers work begin to actively address their external needs? What if individuals feel equipped and empowered to tend to their own internal needs? If staff and administrators work together to abandon the notion that "think of the students!" is an inherently superior mindset, we can adopt the new understanding that "it's not good for the students unless it's good for me, too."

When we make this shift, we begin to see the transformative possibilities for schools that adapt a similar asset model for educators. Just as Developmental Assets decrease negative outcomes and promote positive behaviors in students, an asset framework applied to the staff climate—a framework that would direct its energies toward improving the work life of the educators—has the power to decrease the attitudes and practices that lead to educational burnout.

Using This Book to Change Your School's Dialogue

Is this a book for administrators? *Yes.* Is this a book for teachers? *Yes.* Is this a book for support staff? *Yes.* The beauty of using the eight Developmental Assets categories to focus your thinking is that we're not talking about a program or a curriculum. Anyone can initiate this conversation. There are no prescriptions to follow or hoops to jump through. It can be paperwork-free, organic, and evolving. These concepts are as useful for personal reflection as they are for widespread organizational change.

Whether you want to take stock of your own professional life or start a widespread collaborative effort within your entire school system, use this book to help you engage in two simultaneous inquiries:

- Part I: What are the *external assets* we need to address in order to make this school a more rewarding place to teach?

- Part II: What are the *internal assets* we need to foster in ourselves and in one another in order to make us more fulfilled educators?

Within these sections, you'll find chapters that provide in-depth exploration of each of the asset categories.

As you read through the chapters in this book, you'll find several questions to help you reflect on each concept's relevance to your unique situation. Use these questions to take inventory of your personal experience, or facilitate group discussions to get a wider snapshot of what's going on at your school. Any chapter of this book can be utilized separately to guide staff development trainings or less formal discussions of improved work climate. All of these questions appear in reproducible handout form on the CD-ROM that accompanies this book; print or e-mail handouts to distribute these ideas to all the people you wish to engage in your efforts. If there is a handout available, you'll see a symbol and a label like this:

 [*See handout* **X.X** *on CD-ROM*]

A complete list of handouts and guidelines for usage appears on pages 5–6.

This book is a beginning. More than a book that instructs or directs, this is a book that can prod or inspire you and your colleagues to find tangible ways to improve job satisfaction in your school. This book will provide you the tools and research you need to lead your school and yourself toward a workplace that sustains, renews, and refreshes your commitment to teaching.

Moving toward Hope

As you reflect on the power of this thinking in your own life and in your school, imagine what it is like for students to spend time in a school where teachers feel a lack of support and empowerment. Imagine a school staff that has little or no recognition of the need for boundaries and expectations. Imagine how teachers function when they've lost their sense of positive identity. What is it like being a student in that school or in that classroom?

Now imagine the opposite. Imagine educators working in an environment that fully embraces the need for their professional and personal development. Picture a supportive, empowering climate in which all staff experience collegiality and commitment. Imagine being a student in a school filled with engaged, optimistic teachers.

And what's the first step you can take toward a workplace like this? Look around you, reach out to your colleagues, and listen closely as they respond to this one simple question:

How was *your* day at school?

Notes

1. Scales, P. C. (1996). *Boxed in and bored: How middle schools continue to fail young adolescents and what good middle schools do right.* Minneapolis, MN: Search Institute.

2. Byrne, B. M. (1999). The nomological network of teacher burnout: A literature review and empirically validated model. In R. Vandenberghe & A. M. Huberman (Eds.), *Understanding and preventing teacher burnout: A sourcebook of international research and practice* (p. 55). Cambridge: Cambridge University Press.

3. Freudenberger, H. J. (1974). Staff burnout. *Journal of Social Issues, 30,* 159–165.

Part I:

IDENTIFYING AND BUILDING EXTERNAL ASSETS — THE EXTERNAL STRUCTURES, RELATIONSHIPS, AND ACTIVITIES THAT CREATE A POSITIVE ENVIRONMENT

Whether you seek to identify personal opportunities for improved job satisfaction, collaborate with colleagues on small-group solutions, or lead an entire school district through complex systemic change, it is important to look around you and get the lay of the land. As you read through these first four chapters, consider the following questions:

- *Are* the teachers in your school dissatisfied?
  How do you know?

- What are the specific causes of job dissatisfaction in your school?

- What kinds of changes would you like to see?
  Are the changes you're looking for specific to your experience, or could they apply to your colleagues' situations as well?

- What conversations need to take place to make changes in each of these external categories?

- Who needs to be present for these conversations?
  Who needs to lead?

- Who can help you get started in improving your own job satisfaction?

 [*See handout* **PART 1** *on CD-ROM*]

If you do wish to address external factors collectively, the Center for Teacher Quality (www.calstate.edu/teacherquality) suggests: "To fully understand the problems teachers face in particular schools, the teachers themselves must be asked and must be asked often. Surveys and/or focus groups should be conducted regularly and continuously with all staff, including principals, to assess the quality of the teaching conditions in the school and the district."[1]

Remember that external efforts can have superficial results if they occur without any effort to build internal strengths. Consider the following example:

> *School X decides to recommit a classroom to create a staff lounge in the hopes of providing more opportunities for collegiality among staff. However, this staff room becomes a toxic environment, as teachers simply use the new space for an unhealthy brand of fuming and complaining. Over the course of months, the new staff room becomes relatively vacant and has done little to increase a true sense of collegiality.*

This example illustrates the need for combined external and internal efforts. Collegiality isn't simply a matter of time or space. Collegiality is about *how* the adults work together, not only *where* or *when* they work together. One could argue that without building the internal assets of individual educators, many external attempts at improving work climate could actually be negative or even destructive. For this reason, you'll see personalized questions included throughout the externally focused chapters.

Fortunately for educators and school systems, the cost of asking these questions about work climate, and the corresponding response to the findings, is "often negligible, sometimes little more than a changed mindset (a more collaborative and hopeful attitude)."[2] When you take this positive approach and commit to the importance of improved teacher job satisfaction for yourself and for others, the resulting optimism gives you a tremendous payoff without adding costly policies or procedures.

Notes

1. Futernick, K. (2007). *A possible dream: Retaining California's teachers so all students learn.* Sacramento: California State University. For more information on the Center for Teacher Quality, visit their Web site at www.calstate.edu/teacherquality.

2. Ibid.

CHAPTER ONE: SUPPORT

Staff members feel that they are supportive of, and supported by, their colleagues, administration, and the larger school community.

As an English teacher, I've spent years explaining to students the difference between good writing and fancy language. I try to help them understand that good writing is marked by high standards of creativity and analysis rather than impressive vocabulary or phrasing. I frequently use a disgusting but effective metaphor to make this point. I tell them to picture two cakes. One cake is gorgeous. It consists of three tiers covered in fabulous frosting, flowers, and other decorations. The other cake is rather bland looking. It's a small sheet of cake with a thin layer of plain, brown frosting. So I ask the question: given these two options, which cake would they rather eat?

Once they choose the decorative cake, I resort to pedagogical shock value, informing them that the decorative frosting is really covering a lump of manure. ("EEEEEWW!!!! Mr. EEKKKK-LLLLUUUNNNDDDD!") The plain cake, on the other hand, is actually a delicious, rich chocolate cake.

You and your colleagues are undoubtedly more sophisticated (and probably less interested in manure) than my students, but this is still a useful metaphor for understanding the support that educators need. Think for a moment about the concept of Teacher Appreciation Week. On the one hand, I love donuts and good coffee, and of course I welcome the celebration. But if for just one week out of the year the teachers' lounge is full of treats, does this necessarily represent sincere appreciation? What happens during the other weeks of the year? Is there an overall sense of teacher appreciation in the school, or are these weeks simply the frosting that conceals deeper problems?

There's an alternative possibility here. Even schools that don't have Teacher Appreciation Week—or a nice faculty lounge, or small class sizes, or high salaries—*can* have high levels of support. And this is tremendously important, because—with alarming frequency—**teachers cite lack of administrative and collegial support as their primary reasons for leaving the profession.**[1, 2]

This chapter will explore the various elements of support that are necessary for teachers to remain sustained in the workplace. By the end of this chapter, individuals and school communities will dis-

questions TO CONSIDER

- **Do you experience a** high level of support **from colleagues?**
- **Do you have colleagues to whom you can turn for** professional advice?
- **Do you have colleagues to whom you can turn for** personal advice?
- **How do you show** support **to your colleagues?**
- **Do you feel known and supported by your** administration?
- **Do you see evidence that the** broader community **holds you and your profession in high regard?**
- **Do you feel valued and respected** by students?
- **Do you feel valued and respected** by the parents **of your students?**
- **Do you feel that the structures of your school encourage** collegiality?
- **Do the** people in your personal life **respect and support your work as an educator?**

cover ways to heighten their understanding of and attention to this critical component of job satisfaction.

The Resilience Trap

Before you attempt to increase the experience of support, either for yourself or for the staff at your school, it's helpful to examine your beliefs about resilience. Psychologist Ann Masten refers to resilience as the "ordinary magic" that allows individuals to protect themselves and overcome challenges.[3] While there are many definitions of resilience, it will probably best serve this conversation to think of resilience as our ability to bounce back from trials and disappointments and to cope with our ongoing stresses. Certainly resilience is critical to effective teaching, and it should be emphasized as a key element of good staff relations and personal strength; however, an exclusive focus on resilience can be counterproductive to institutional—or external—change. To put it bleakly, a school that offers resilience training without making other changes may imply the following message: *We'll provide training for you to increase your resilience, but we will ignore the conditions that make resilience difficult.*

As an illustration of the "resilience trap," consider the following scenario: You've been working too hard for too long. You've strung together days upon days of late nights and early mornings, just trying to keep up with the demands of your work and life. You recognize that you're exhausted. So for one glorious night, you decide not to grade or plan or stress about the next day. In fact, you go and get a massage. Then you go to see a movie. And for that one night you go to bed early and get a good, long, sound night of sleep. In the morning you head back to work, refreshed and energized. Fast-forward two weeks. Has that one night actually made a difference in your long-term energy levels and happiness? Did your genuine efforts at resilience actually change the experience of burnout for yourself, or were those moments of peace simply swirls of frosting on top of the cake, looking nice but doing little to address underlying issues? At the end of the day, we don't just want resilient adults working in unhealthy environments. We want healthy, resilient adults working in healthy, supportive environments.

The point is, resilience is essential when people need to deal with and overcome negative conditions, but the negative conditions also require attention. Obviously it's not always possible to simply remove the obstacles. This is where support comes in. Feeling supported means *knowing that you're not alone*. So what happens if we abandon the pitfalls of individual resilience in exchange for collective resilience?

We Just Want a Sandwich!

Support comes in many forms, and I was reminded of this when I visited a high school staff to help them work through some professional development issues. As we discussed day-to-day obstacles they faced, several of the teachers reported ongoing frustration about the fact that by the time they got to the lunchroom to eat, there was no food left for them. So amid difficult discussions about achievement gaps, school safety, and long-range district planning, these educators voiced a much simpler plea: *we just want a sandwich!*

Before we got started on the larger discussions about the very real challenges facing the school, the group contemplated solutions to this smaller but extremely frustrating concern. Staff were talking together about the annoyance rather than suffering quietly or griping informally. Once they felt the support of the group, it was easy to arrive at a simple solution to their problem: Each day in the main office, there would be a sign-up sheet for teachers who were planning to eat in the cafeteria. The kitchen staff would then set aside lunches on a separate cart for the teachers so they would be assured that, at the very least, they would have food to eat. Problem solved.

To a great degree, conversations like these are dependent on a staff's ability to question what they've come to accept as reality. To accept that "this is always how we've done it" or "this is just the way it is" is to believe that change isn't possible. When you want to change something about your workplace, you must cast aside that kind of thinking. But here's the trick: Individuals rarely feel powerful enough to change reality. For this reason, building support can be a fruitful first step when you're working to improve teacher job satisfaction. Simply making time and space for dialogue is one major leap toward the solution to any problem.

Strengthening Collegiality through Mentoring

Before we can build stronger support among educators, we need to foster trust and collegiality. Because the demands of education are too profound to grapple with in isolation, we must seek to build and sustain relationships that support us emotionally, personally, and professionally in our teaching. One way you can do this is by making a core commitment to yourself and to your colleagues:

We are each other's mentors.

Many school districts have actively formalized the mentorship process for new teachers in an effort to help inexperienced teachers through the initial stages of their careers. Mentors help ensure that young teachers receive the support they need to develop their teaching skills and create positive impressions of their profession. Unfortunately, such programs are usually finite, spanning only the early years of a teacher's career. What happens after those first years of teaching? No matter how many years one teaches, the challenges do not go away. In fact, as teachers take on more responsibilities and as the potential fatigue and disillusionment of multiple years of teaching settle in, the need for mentoring and strong collegial relationships actually increases.

Mentoring is a particularly powerful strategy for building collegiality because it can happen informally, at the personal level, or formally, at an institutional level. Whether or not your school promotes mentoring, the first step toward collegial support must be a personal commitment to each other. You can make this commitment by adopting the following statements:

I need the support of other adults and cannot do this work by myself.

I must make the time to support other adults in this work.

This outlook motivates you to accept personal responsibility for developing collegiality and sources of support in your own work life, and also connects you to others in your school. The difference between making isolated personal efforts at resilience and building a true network of support becomes apparent when you adopt the latter approach.

How Was *Your* Day at School?

At Russell Middle School in Millard, Nebraska, the social e-mails went out to the whole staff. Several of the female colleagues at the school were getting together for stitching clubs. Or sometimes they spent time scrapbooking together. A social life was part of the staff climate—for the women.

But what about the men? Although they hadn't been intentionally excluded, they had nothing similar to support them in their work life. Randy Langdon decided to do something to remedy the situation. He and his male colleagues weren't necessarily interested in pursuing the same kinds of hobbies together, but they did want to feel a similar sense of connection and collegiality. He proposed a weekly Men's Club. The idea took off immediately, and Randy continues to meet with his male colleagues every week.

Men's Club is an open, standing invitation for all male staff members. They meet every Friday at 6:30 a.m., gathering at a restaurant within a local grocery store. The agenda is simple: Come and drink coffee. Talk about life, family—whatever. This is just a chance to be together and wrap up the week.

The women see how valuable this outlet is to their colleagues. They have threatened to crash the party one of these weeks, but they haven't—yet.

[*See handout* **1.1** *on CD-ROM*]

PERSONAL INVENTORY

The items below describe frequent themes that arise in Search Institute's staff development trainings with educators. Use these items to reflect on your own experience of support.

You *feel supported by* your colleagues:

	STRONGLY DISAGREE	DISAGREE	NOT SURE	AGREE	STRONGLY AGREE
I can name a small group of teachers to whom I can turn for advice and support on a variety of issues.					
I can name at least one colleague who mentors me, either formally or informally.					
I can name at least one colleague who inspires me to become a better teacher.					
I can and do ask my colleagues for help.					
Staff members know my skills and capabilities.					
Staff members offer to help me without my asking.					

You *are supportive of* your colleagues:

	STRONGLY DISAGREE	DISAGREE	NOT SURE	AGREE	STRONGLY AGREE
I can name a small group of teachers to whom I feel responsible.					
I ask these colleagues how they are doing at least once a week.					
I try to be a mentor to at least one colleague, either formally or informally.					
I offer to help when a colleague has a problem.					

[*See handout* **1.2** *on CD-ROM*]

INSTITUTIONAL INVENTORY

Use this checklist to identify the ways that your school is already experiencing strong support among staff.

	STRONGLY DISAGREE	DISAGREE	NOT SURE	AGREE	STRONGLY AGREE
Our school has practices or procedures that foster collegiality for both personal and professional growth.					
An atmosphere of collegiality is built into our in-service trainings and professional development activities.					
Our staff members have time to connect informally each day.					
Our school has a formal mentoring arrangement that connects each staff person to at least one other staff person.					
Our administration understands the value of colleagues spending time together.					
Our staff members value collegiality.					
Our staff members ask for help when they need it.					

Putting Support into Action

If you've already identified a strong sense of collegiality among the staff at your school, or you've spent time reaching out informally to your coworkers, you're ready to harness the power of supportive professional relationships when talking about teacher job satisfaction. First, convene a group of staff members to begin this conversation. Use the "Now What Do I Do?" questions on page 38 to facilitate a conversation that focuses on your school's strengths—the things you're already doing right. Beginning with positive observations will give your conversation momentum and help you identify the opportunities you already have to tackle problems.

Next, name the obstacles that prevent teachers from experiencing job satisfaction. This list should be detailed, not full of generalities. Include all observations—regardless of how small they may seem—that stand between you and your sense of success and joy as an educator. If joy seems like a stretch, it is useful to note what Joan Lipsitz revealed in her groundbreaking book *Successful Schools for Young Adolescents*: "Laughter, vitality, interest, smiles, and other indications of pleasure are reasonable expectations for schools." She contends that joy is "nonnegotiable," and that "happy experiences in school are central to well-being and should be so recognized by policy setters, practitioners, and researchers."[4] Adopt a similarly "nonnegotiable" policy toward your own joy as you make this list.

Remind your group that nothing within your present reality has to stay exactly as it is. If the condition or obstacle itself cannot change, you can change how you approach or respond to the issue.

Now that you have one long, discouraging list of impossible grievances, STOP. Remind the group that you're in this together. Then choose one thing you're going to do differently. One small, manageable, concrete success is a powerful thing. Even if you simply figure out how to get everyone a sandwich, you're on your way to improving the work climate at your school.

 [*See handout* **1.3** *on CD-ROM*]

CHAPTER 1:
SHIFTING FROM ISOLATION TO SUPPORT

If you noticed an isolated or forlorn student, chances are you'd try to become involved and explore what you could do to help. However, chances are equally good that you might feel reluctant to do the same with colleagues. You may feel even *more* reluctant to be the one who asks for help. Consider the following shifts as you work to build support in your workplace:

ISOLATING YOURSELF FROM SOURCES OF SUPPORT	BUILDING A NETWORK OF SUPPORT
If I ask for help, I might appear needy or deficient in my work.	If I don't ask for help, I can't do my job as well.
If I ask for help, I might be burdening someone who is already overburdened.	I need help from others to prevent burnout and to remain motivated and inspired.

continued

ISOLATING YOURSELF FROM SOURCES OF SUPPORT	BUILDING A NETWORK OF SUPPORT
I'm so busy that I don't have time to help someone else.	Lending support can energize me and reminds me that I can ask for support when I need it.
I'm sure my colleague can solve problems without my help.	Even if my colleague has things under control, everyone appreciates knowing they're not alone.
If I offer help, the other person may feel as if I'm being critical.	If I needed help, I would appreciate receiving it from my colleagues.

 [*See handout* 1.4 *on CD-ROM*]

NOW WHAT DO I DO?
MOVING IDEAS TO ACTION

The following questions are intended to give you concrete steps you can use to turn the ideas in this chapter into actions in your own life and work. If you are working with a large group, you may find it useful to break into pairs or smaller groups for discussion. Whether you pursue these actions as an administrator on the institutional level or as a colleague reaching out to coworkers, you have the power to start increasing the experience of support in your school.

1. Schedule an informal discussion for staff interested in exploring teacher job satisfaction at your school. Ask participants to discuss the following questions:

   a. What motivates and unites teachers and staff at our school?
   b. What is going well for our staff?
   c. What opportunities do we have to communicate?
   d. What support systems does our school have in place?

2. Next ask participants to identify the ongoing, recurring frustrations that keep them from feeling fully engaged with their work. Choose *one* of these frustrations to facilitate a deeper discussion, asking the following questions:

a. What individual steps can each person take to remove or lessen this obstacle?

b. What group opportunities or systems of support already exist to address this problem?

c. How can we better support each other in our individual efforts to address this frustration?

3. Now identify one aspect of your workplace environment that could be categorized by the phrase, "We've always done it this way." Ask these questions:

a. Which elements of this approach still seem logical or reasonable in our present workplace?

b. Which elements of this approach are no longer helpful?

c. What is one concrete, *collective* measure we can take to rethink this practice?

Making It Personal

In addition to the group efforts described above, make a personal commitment to increasing support in your workplace:

1. Name one teacher who you know could use increased support in her/his work at school. Identify one concrete step you could take to extend this support:

2. Name one of your present roles/tasks that you do not feel you are completing to your own satisfaction. Identify one colleague who could be an ally, giving you the support you need to better fulfill this duty:

Notes

1. Futernick, K. (2007). *A possible dream: Retaining California's teachers so all students learn.* Sacramento: California State University.

2. MetLife. (2005). *MetLife survey of the American teacher: Transitions and the role of supportive relationships.* Markow, D., Martin, S.

3. Masten, A. S. (2001). Ordinary magic. Resilience processes in development. *The American Psychologist, 56*(3), 227–38.

4. Lipsitz, J. (1984). *Successful schools for young adolescents.* New Brunswick, NJ: Transaction Books (p. 15).

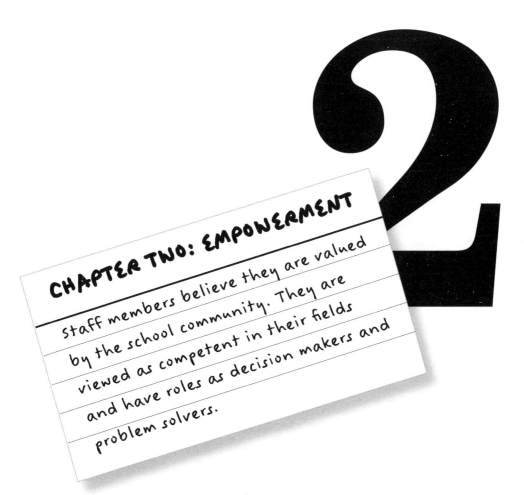

CHAPTER TWO: EMPOWERMENT

Staff members believe they are valued by the school community. They are viewed as competent in their fields and have roles as decision makers and problem solvers.

In Chapter 1 we explored the ways in which collegiality and support make it possible for you and your colleagues to work together toward the changes you wish to see. As you identify the small and large actions you can take to effect change, you'll also start to experience empowerment. Consider the following scenario:

A high school English department has 10 teachers. Overall, support is strong in this group, and they work well together; however, they face challenges and concerns just as any other group of colleagues does. One of the most pressing tensions concerns meeting grading deadlines. On one side is a group of teachers who grade and return 70 or so essays within a day or two of receiving them. While greatly appreciated by the students and parents, this quick turnaround takes a tremendous toll on the teachers, who accomplish this feat by staying up nearly all night—and come to work exhausted and stressed the next day. On the other side is a group of teachers whose paper-grading time nears a month. These teachers may be well rested and relaxed, but their students complain about the delayed grading.

The disparity in work habits eventually creates tension within the department, because the "one nighters" are frustrated that their efforts are not matched by their colleagues', while the "one monthers" feel they are being accused of laziness, and that students' expectations have been set too high by the quick turnaround. Each group feels some degree of resentment, and also feels powerless to affect the behavior of the other group.

Because these colleagues otherwise share a strong sense of collegiality, they are able to hold a frank discussion about the problem at a department meeting, seeking a middle ground that is fair to both the teachers and their students. After some good conversation and a little bargaining, the department agrees to a new turnaround time for paper grading. They write up a group contract, signed by the teachers and distributed to the students, committing to a one-week turnaround. As a result, the "one nighters" are less exhausted, and the "one monthers" perform more responsibly.

Group solutions and teamwork are possible when staff members feel empowered to solve problems together rather than suffering silently. This chapter explores how educators can become more involved in shaping their own professional practices. When all staff members have a voice and share ownership, they are better able to reach the personal, professional, and academic goals of teaching.

questions
TO CONSIDER

○ **Do you experience a feeling of** appreciation **in your workplace?**

○ **Do you and your colleagues use each other as** resources?

○ **Are all staff members in your school** consulted about decisions **that affect them?**

○ **Do staff members and administrators communicate about concerns, new ideas, and other opportunities to** improve your school?

○ **How do administrators** communicate necessary feedback and information **to staff?**

○ **Are there areas in which you are able to make your own decisions and given administrative support for** exercising your own judgment?

The goal of this chapter is to evaluate how you and your colleagues share control over professional decisions and problem solving. Being a valued participant in decision making is crucial to your happiness and success in teaching. Without a prevailing sense of empowerment, it is difficult to feel included and effective in the workplace.

Bringing Teachers and Administrators Together

Perhaps no relationship in a school setting is as important as that between staff and administration. Fundamental breakdowns in these relationships affect the entire school climate. Staff and administration can put significant pressure on each other because of competing desires or goals, but they still share a symbiotic relationship. An administrator cannot succeed without an effective teaching staff. Staff members cannot succeed without effective leadership. Although a host of issues can lead to tension between the two parties, they depend on each other for a successful work environment. Because this relationship is a key intersection in a school's work climate, job satisfaction can be seriously jeopardized when this connection suffers.

A communication breakdown between staff and administration is one of the most common obstacles to empowerment. In fact, hierarchies of any kind (at the district, building, or department level) have the potential to make people feel disenfranchised, powerless, or undervalued. This is not to suggest that hierarchy is *always* a barrier to empowerment; on the contrary, people working higher up in power structures are in a unique position to share decision making, while people working in lower-level positions can be informal leaders, speaking up on behalf of themselves and their colleagues.

Whether you are working as an administrator or a classroom teacher, you can shift your thinking away from an adversarial approach; doing so has the potential to transform the quality of relationships in the workplace. However large or small your sphere of influence, you can respond to your colleagues in a way that helps them feel valued, respected, and knowledgeable.

Empowerment on an Individual Level

Think back to the story about grading deadlines that opened this chapter. That situation was real, and it involved a small group of teachers who became serious about improving their own work climate. They faced a tangible problem and sat down to solve it together—without the involvement of an outside mediator, administrator, or consultant.

In a study led by Ken Futernick from the Center for Teacher Quality, titled *A Possible Dream: Retaining California Teachers So All Students Learn,* more than 2,000 educators provided key insights into why some were "leavers" and others were "stayers" in the profession. The basic finding in this study was that:

> Teachers are less concerned with compensation (though they are not unconcerned with it) than they are with a whole range of particulars about their work environment. Work environment, or perhaps more specifically described *the teaching and learning environment*, refers not just to leaks in the ceilings or toilets that do not flush, though poorly maintained classrooms and school facilities are as dispiriting to teachers as they are to students. Teaching and learning environment refers to a whole range of instructional, collegial, and systemic conditions which, for many, make teaching a highly satisfying profession. A profession that reminds those who have chosen it that they are making a positive impact on students and society.[1]

The report paints a picture of teachers who are struggling with inadequate support from their district or administration and are drowning in bureaucratic minutiae. As Futernick states, "These problematic 'facts of life,' assumed by many to be unavoidable, do not just drive teachers crazy; they drive many of them right out of the classroom."[2] Put simply, if teachers wait for their conditions to improve, or if they accept that "this is just how things are," they may not be able to sustain themselves for long.

Certainly, schools can make widespread, institutional changes from the top down. But when you adopt a strength-based approach of empowerment, you don't have to wait for that to happen. This is do-it-yourself job satisfaction.

This is not about being entirely self-reliant and resilient, solving all your problems by yourself. This is about looking around, connecting with colleagues, and identifying opportunities. Use the personal inventory on page 45 to think about the ways you can start to improve your work climate.

[*See handout* **2.1** *on CD-ROM*]

PERSONAL INVENTORY

The items below describe frequent themes that arise in Search Institute's staff development trainings with educators. Use these items to reflect on your own experience of empowerment.

You *feel empowered:*

	STRONGLY DISAGREE	DISAGREE	NOT SURE	AGREE	STRONGLY AGREE
I frequently have opportunities to voice my opinion about decisions that affect me.					
I feel the school and the community hold my profession in high regard.					
My colleagues and I are consulted before final decisions are made that affect our teaching.					
I feel respected and valued by my students.					
I feel respected by my colleagues.					
My colleagues use me as a resource.					
I have the means to grow professionally.					

You *empower others:*

	STRONGLY DISAGREE	DISAGREE	NOT SURE	AGREE	STRONGLY AGREE
I share problem solving and decision making with my colleagues.					
I seek colleagues' input about important matters affecting workplace conditions.					
I respect the professional judgment of the decision makers in the school.					
I see myself as a partner with my colleagues in carrying out a broader mission beyond my classroom performance.					

Empowerment on an Administrative Level

When you're working from an administrative perspective, it's important to develop both a culture and a system that actively seeks teacher input about working conditions. California State University's Center for Teacher Quality recommends the following strategies to empower individuals in the process of being instructive and reflective about the workplace environment:

- Human resources personnel should conduct exit interviews and/or surveys with teachers who leave the profession or transfer to other schools.

- Surveys and/or focus groups should be conducted regularly and continuously with all staff, including site administrators, to assess the quality of school district working conditions.

- Teachers should be invited to participate in the analysis of findings and in the development of plans to improve teaching and learning conditions.

- Efforts to improve teaching and learning conditions should be evaluated and adjusted.

- These assessments should be conducted annually.[3]

TRUE STORY

How Was *Your* Day at School?

Education uses a pretty standard hierarchy of evaluation and feedback: teachers evaluate students, and administrators evaluate teachers. But when Addie Kaufman began her career as an assistant principal, she was surprised to learn that her superintendent had initiated a more unusual practice: the teachers evaluated the administrators.

Now a principal, Addie also uses an "Administrator Report Card" to gather feedback about her performance and collect staff input on new directions for the school.

This evaluation uses several "on a scale from 1 to 10" questions and the following essay questions:

- What are my strengths?
- In what areas would you like to see me improve?
- As I set my goals for next year, on what should I concentrate?

Staff members complete this report card as one of their end-of-the-year checkout responsibilities. All feedback is anonymous, and staff members are welcome to type their responses if they don't want anyone to recognize their handwriting. The results are then compiled for Addie and her assistant principals so they can reflect on staff responses. Addie uses staff feedback to create her personal goals for the following school year—goals she shares with staff and her own superiors.

The reaction from staff has been tremendous: they appreciate the courage and transparency necessary for administrators to accept this degree of scrutiny. By participating, staff members share accountability for schoolwide progress and improvement.

A forthright process such as this does come with a degree of friction, of course. As Addie points out, "Remember that teachers at the end of the year are tired and sometimes angry. They may write some nasty things. You can't take the comments personally, and there's no point in sitting there and trying to figure out who wrote what."

What advice does Addie have for other administrators who wish to try this strategy? First, write meaningful survey questions with which you feel comfortable. When teachers respond with thought and honesty, accept the feedback as useful information, identifying areas for improvement. Follow up on the suggestions you receive, and monitor your progress. Communicate results with staff, and share in the process of good conversation and tough decisions.

[*See handout* **2.2** *on CD-ROM*]

INSTITUTIONAL INVENTORY

Use this checklist to identify the ways that your school is already experiencing empowerment among staff.

	STRONGLY DISAGREE	DISAGREE	NOT SURE	AGREE	STRONGLY AGREE
Our school considers all staff as decision makers.					
Our staff members are mindful of how we treat one another.					
Colleagues in my school call on each other as resources.					
Staff generally defer to one another in a respectful manner when necessary.					
Staff are able to criticize a work condition without fear of reprisal.					
Staff have time to pursue opportunities to collaborate with one another.					
The school provides adequate resources necessary for professional development and classroom endeavors.					

Putting Empowerment into Action

Empowerment refers to the prevailing sense that you have some degree of control over what you are doing, a notion called *self-efficacy*. This is also closely linked with a positive identity, which we'll explore further in Chapter 8. With respect to empowerment, self-efficacy means you feel valued and have safe opportunities to meaningfully contribute. Whether you address this concern on a personal level or at the institutional level, it is helpful to know a little more about how self-efficacy works. Psychologist Albert Bandura suggests that there are four sources of self-efficacy. A paraphrased version appears below:

Enactive mastery experiences Positive outcomes to challenging experiences will increase self-efficacy, while outcomes perceived as failures will lower this sense of personal power. Experiences that are not sufficiently challenging or are easy to accomplish do little to hone one's sense of control over one's life.

Vicarious experiences These are observations of others who experience success in a similar setting. Seeing others achieve through diligence and perseverance increases an individual's sense that a similar personal effort will likewise lead to success. Watching others fail after sustained effort can lower one's sense of efficacy.

Persuasive communication This is a form of social persuasion in which individuals are encouraged in the belief that they can make decisions and exercise control over their lives. Persuasive communication is most valuable when those who deliver the message are viewed as competent and reliable.

Physiological responses The emotional and physical responses of individuals to their surroundings and events can be indicators of self-efficacy. In a sense this refers to the way it "feels" to be empowered.[4]

Clearly, the conversation about the way you view yourself, your work, your colleagues, and your own sense of empowerment in your life is intricate and multifaceted. Defining your professional self is based on your own and others' perception of your success and abilities.

Then there is the larger journey of defining one's identity and self-worth. For teachers, the line between these two perceptions is usually thin. When you say, "I am a teacher," chances are you have blurred the line between saying "This is what I do for a living" and "This is who I am." This level of commitment is a central reason why many educators excel; however, self-efficacy becomes an even greater challenge when professional success is so deeply connected to overall personal identity. This makes the experience of empowerment even more crucial to the job satisfaction of educators.

From Bandura's perspective, one of the most critical steps to take in this evolution toward personal power is to experience hard-won success. It's critical that the challenges we pose ourselves require exertion and perseverance; it's not enough to tackle simple measures of improvement. In fact, Bandura notes:

> If people experience only easy successes, they come to expect quick results and are easily discouraged by failure. A resilient sense of efficacy requires experience in overcoming obstacles

through perseverant effort. Some setbacks and difficulties in human pursuits serve a useful purpose in teaching that success usually requires sustained effort. After people become convinced they have what it takes to succeed, they persevere in the face of adversity and quickly rebound from setbacks. By sticking it out through tough times, they emerge stronger from adversity."[5]

Therefore, it's critical that as individuals develop their own heightened sense of personal control and power, they continue to seek meaningful challenges.

Consider the "Opportunities for Empowerment" exercise below as you think through these ideas. Focus solely on your professional life as you fill in the four categories.

 [*See handout* **2.3** *on CD-ROM*]

OPPORTUNITIES FOR EMPOWERMENT

Short-term, immediate, and "EASY" obstacles or goals (e.g., cleaning your desk):	Short-term, immediate, and "DIFFICULT" obstacles or goals (e.g., resolving a lingering conflict with a colleague):
Long-term, sustainable, and "EASY" obstacles or goals (e.g., establishing shared expectations for the turnaround time on grading):	Long-term, sustainable, and "DIFFICULT" obstacles or goals (e.g., restructuring professional development):

Short-term potential successes include such tasks as cleaning your desk, returning backlogged e-mails, or finishing lingering grading. The successful completion of any of these tasks serves to actively remove stress and guilt from your daily life, and accomplishing these sorts of tasks goes a long way toward fulfilling some of the other more important elements and values of your work. Getting into the habit of picking this low-hanging fruit is a great source of relief, and certainly reflects the diligence we encourage with our students, but to establish true efficacy, push yourself to take action in all four quadrants of this table.

As you move to the discussion of boundaries in Chapter 3, remember how valuable self-efficacy can be. Discovering and creating opportunities for empowerment will enable you to accomplish many of the other efforts described in the chapters that follow.

 [*See handout* **2.4** *on CD-ROM*]

CHAPTER 2:
SHIFTING FROM DEFEAT TO EMPOWERMENT

Consider the following shifts as you work to become empowered in your workplace:

FEELING POWERLESS	BECOMING EMPOWERED
Our school lacks the resources to make the change I'd like to see.	I will identify at least one thing I can do differently today to take a step toward this change.
Difficulties and complaints seem to be constant in my work experience.	Difficulties and complaints are opportunities for improvement.
I have little say in the decisions that affect my work.	Instead of battling individual decisions, I can work to create systems and a culture that ensures my voice is heard.
No matter how many times I cite the same frustration, nothing seems to change.	I will not leave a meeting or end a conversation until I've identified a concrete initial step toward improvement.

[*See handout* **2.5** *on CD-ROM*]

NOW WHAT DO I DO?
MOVING IDEAS TO ACTION

One area of my work life I want more control over:

1–3 obstacles I will need to overcome to do this:

1.

2.

3.

The first step I can take to address one of these obstacles:

The date by which I will take this first step:

One staff person I can ask to be my goal partner*:

> * A goal partner is someone with whom you share your goal,
> review the obstacles, and discuss strategies for overcoming the
> obstacles, who agrees to check in with you about your progress
> and holds you accountable to yourself to take action—and who
> celebrates your successes with you.

Understanding and Expanding Your Influence

Think about the area of your work life you described above. As you set
goals and take power into your own hands, consider the following:

These are the things I *do* have the power to control in this scenario:

What can I do with this power?

These are the things I wish I could control, but don't feel I have the
power to influence:

Who *does* have the power to influence these things?

How do I currently communicate with the people who influence this set of decisions?

What additional opportunities do I have to communicate with these decision makers?

When and where are teachers and administrators already meeting to make the decisions that affect me? How do I contribute a voice there?

How might I use those opportunities better?

Oftentimes staff members are invited to weigh in on a decision, but they feel excluded during the communication and implementation phases.

- How much information do you get about the decisions that affect you? How might you gain access to more information?

- What role do you play in the implementation of school policies and practices? How might you find a more active role for yourself in the implementation phase?

Notes

1. Futernick, K. (2007). *A possible dream: Retaining California's teachers so all students learn.* Sacramento: California State University. For more information on the Center for Teacher Quality, visit their Web site at www.calstate.edu/teacherquality.

2. Ibid.

3. Ibid.

4. Bandura, A. (1994). Self-efficacy [Electronic version]. In V. S. Ramachaudran (Ed.), *Encyclopedia of human behavior* (Vol. 4, pp. 71–81). New York: Academic Press.

5. Ibid.

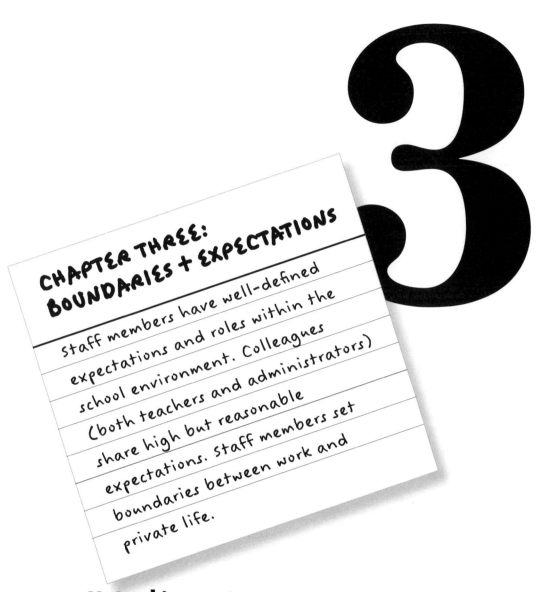

CHAPTER THREE: BOUNDARIES + EXPECTATIONS

Staff members have well-defined expectations and roles within the school environment. Colleagues (both teachers and administrators) share high but reasonable expectations. Staff members set boundaries between work and private life.

My teaching mentor was a man named Tom Leuchtenberg. He was a wonderfully joyful theater/English teacher with a flamboyant personality. Tom eased me into teaching with an air of pleasure and freedom that affected the way I taught from the day I met him. Each time I saw him in the hall, I'd ask, "How are you, Tom?"

He'd always reply, "Better than I have any right to be." It wasn't just a glib answer. He meant it. Joyful teaching was a way of life for him.

I walked past Tom's classroom on the way out to my car each night. I was 22 years old and trying to prove myself to the staff and my students. Often this meant carrying home boxes and boxes of extra work and papers to grade each night. Whenever he'd see me

questions TO CONSIDER

○ **Are your school's expectations of you** clear **and** reasonable?

○ **Do you and your colleagues value a** balance **between work life and personal life?**

○ **Do you protect your own** boundaries? **Do you respect your colleagues' boundaries?**

○ **Does your school's work culture** support or undermine **reasonable boundaries for educators?**

so burdened, he'd lean out his window and bellow, "What's wrong, Nathan? We don't pay you enough to work during the day?"

Tom was instrumental in teaching me to set my own limits. Since the school and its systems weren't necessarily going to set limits for me, I had to set them for myself. I don't remember learning a huge amount of pedagogy or classroom management from Tom, but I cherish the influence he had on making me a happy teacher. Tom gave me the foundation I needed in order to maintain high but reasonable expectations for myself while setting manageable boundaries.

Role Call: Which Hat Am I Wearing?

The life of a teacher is a rewarding but daunting one. The ubiquitous term "teacher" does little to encompass all that makes up a year of teaching. To more accurately depict the full extent of the work you do, read through the following list and note how many of these roles you play on any given day:

- Planner
- Grader
- Nurturer
- Writer
- Speaker
- Nurse
- Police officer
- Counselor
- Department chair
- Club advisor
- Curriculum writer
- Coach
- Colleague

And the list doesn't end there. With parents you sometimes need to be a politician. With students you sometimes need to serve as judge and jury. With colleagues you can act as a psychologist. And in the classroom you can be a parent, a comedian, and a scholar all at once. The many hats we wear are part of what makes being a teacher so overwhelmingly satisfying—and exhausting.

None of this is news to an educator. Few teachers arrive at school in the morning to teach and then leave immediately after the bell rings. Part of being a teacher means seeking ways in which you can better reach your students and further fulfill the altruistic goals with which you entered the profession. Teachers who go above and beyond the stated job description are, and often should be, held up as models of excellence. The trouble is, wearing too many hats at once can make your head hurt.

When you see a young person who is spread too thin, a Super Student who has excellent grades and is involved in sports, arts, and school leadership, what concerns do you have for her? You're afraid that in her attempt to be a "successful" student she might also be denying herself the pleasure of simply being a learner and enjoying the experience of childhood or young adulthood. You are likely to have thoughtful discussions with this young person about making positive choices to conserve her time and energy, perhaps even suggesting that she step back from some of her activities. You do this because, above all, you know that being happy and healthy is an important part of being successful.

But do we apply this same wisdom to our own lives? Why do we encourage this broader sense of personal health and satisfaction for students but fail to heed our own advice?

Setting Boundaries to Prevent Burnout

The deep sense of commitment described above comes at a tremendous personal price to educators. And sadly, the risk is usually greatest among the Super Teachers—those who fill every possible role in an effort to pursue the highest goals and ideals of education. Researcher Bernd Rudow writes, "In general, only the teacher who is 'burning' can 'burn out.' Teachers subject to burnout are those who are involved, devoted, and conscientious. Their involvement is determined by social caring and selfless motives, which make up the personal purpose of the job."[1] These are teachers like you who perhaps entered the profession not only with a love of the content they deliver, but also for the young people to whom they've dedicated their lives and careers. Rudow points out that there is a troubling irony in the fact that a teacher who is so deeply invested in the lives of students runs the highest risk of burning out. Some researchers argue that burnout comes from without, as a direct result of external, organizational stressors, while others contend that burnout comes from within, when an individual copes with unsatisfactory working conditions by taking on more responsibility.[2,3] Either way, it is clear that **any decrease in workplace satisfaction is accompanied by an increased risk of burnout.** These two possible causes of burnout suggest two accompanying sets of solutions:

1. Better school support for healthy boundaries among staff members, and

2. Better individual decision making to establish personal boundaries.

This dual approach is powerful because it identifies burnout as a shared problem between teachers and administrators. When both groups take responsibility for finding solutions, there is a much greater chance that staff members will experience clear boundaries and high expectations.

Setting Boundaries on a Personal Level

One of the fastest ways to start setting your own boundaries is to take stock of the many roles you play. As you delve into this process, ask yourself whether or not you can continue on your present trajectory. Are you on a sustainable, long-term path? How much trouble are you having getting through this week? This semester? This school year?

There is and always will be an element of survival in teaching. At times educators are simply making decisions that will allow them to get through a single day. That's the nature of the work. The trouble comes when these "survival" days become a constant way of life, progressing to higher and higher levels of stress. Consider the concept of Boiling Frog Syndrome: If you throw a frog into a pot of boiling water, it will immediately jump out to save itself; however, if you place a frog in cold water and then slowly increase the heat, the frog will stay in the water, ultimately boiling to death.

You may have started your career with a reasonable workload, but as you take on more roles and more responsibilities, the water in which you swim does indeed get a little warmer. And the less you pay attention to this increase, the warmer you allow the water to become. And warmer. And warmer. And warmer. Until?

Of course, you are not a hapless frog. Instead, you can change your roles and control your situation to alter the water in which you swim—but only if you're paying attention to the temperature.

Conquering Role Ambiguity

Research shows that role ambiguity is one leading cause of burnout among educators.[4] Sometimes two or more roles may be in conflict with one another; complying with one set of pressures makes compliance with the other set more difficult.[5] For example, the responsibilities of coaching an after-school sport compete with the responsibilities of grading homework. Whenever multiple roles compete for time and energy, teachers are at risk for exhaustion and burnout.

Educators must carefully choose the various roles that they will play in the operations of a school. As mentioned earlier, simply being a classroom teacher comes with a long list of responsibilities. Each new class a teacher takes on requires additional content knowledge and preparatory time. Add to that list roles of leadership such as coordinating a team or serving on district planning committees. It is important to note that all of these roles can be important, fulfilling, and even fun. But every time you take on a new role, you set more goals for yourself and become accountable to another group of people. And the more functions you have, the more likely you are to feel that you're not fulfilling *any* of the roles to your own standards. Instead of feeling challenged and energized by these rich experiences, many educators are left saddened, frustrated, and near exhaustion.

But there is a hopeful side to this discussion as well. Taking on new roles can increase your opportunities to contribute to the school and your sense of mission. Learning new roles can allow you to develop skills and make new relationships with others. All of these increases can lead you to a stronger sense of accomplishment. This means that you shouldn't simply say no to everything, minimizing your involvement in the life of the school, but rather find a healthy mix of clear, rewarding roles that sustain you as an educator.

Reflect on the table called "My Professional Roles" below. As you fill in these boxes, think only about your work life, not the roles of your personal life. In the last box, try to figure out what portion of your time you give to each role.

 [*See handout* **3.1** *on CD-ROM*]

MY PROFESSIONAL ROLES

ROLE (e.g., teacher, coach, theater director)	RESPONSIBLE TO WHOM?	PRIMARY TASKS AND DUTIES	PERSONAL SATISFACTION PROVIDED BY SERVING THIS ROLE	% OF TOTAL TIME AND ENERGY GIVEN TO THIS ROLE WEEKLY

Note that the table only provides three spaces for your roles. How many spaces did you want? What does that indicate about your own professional responsibilities? To how many different groups of people are you truly responsible? How many duties do you have? How many do you fulfill successfully? To what extent does each role make you happier or more engaged in your work? Which roles burden you and make your life less enjoyable? And how much of yourself are you able to give while playing all of these roles?

⟹ [*See handout* **3.1** *on CD-ROM*]

MY PERSONAL ROLES

ROLE (e.g., spouse, parent)	RESPONSIBLE TO WHOM?	PRIMARY TASKS AND DUTIES	PERSONAL SATISFACTION PROVIDED BY SERVING THIS ROLE	% OF TOTAL TIME AND ENERGY GIVEN TO THIS ROLE WEEKLY

This table was purposeful about limiting your thinking only to your work life. Now refer to the table called "My Personal Roles" above, this time thinking only of the roles you play outside of work.

Phew. Exhausted yet? Taken together, the two tables most likely just scratch the surface of your present responsibilities. But it's important to step back and gain some perspective on how you are *fed* by these roles and how you *can* keep yourself sane and sustained, whether you have willingly embraced these obligations or have had them foisted upon you.

We tell others, "You can't be all things to all people," but we don't always do such a stellar job of reminding ourselves of this truth. What might change if we instead adopt the attitude, "I can be a lot of things to a lot of people," or, "I can be very good at a few things for some people"? These sentences are less heroic and grandiose than those we usually utter about our work, but by narrowing your focus to the roles that matter most, you can make your work more effective.

Examining *what* roles we play, as well as *how* we fill those roles, is worth exploring. It's not difficult to imagine the direct connection between "I'm not really myself when I'm in this role," and "I don't like this role." Examining the distance between a particular role and your ability to fulfill that role is one way to measure whether or not the role is sustainable. Use the table called "Does the Role Fit?" below as a starting point for you to begin reimagining the roles you play and how you play them.

 [*See handout* **3.1** *on CD-ROM*]

DOES THE ROLE FIT?

TITLE OF ROLE:	How my personality, beliefs, and strengths serve this role well:	How this role conflicts with my personality, beliefs, or strengths:	Steps I can take to make the role closer to my true self:

Whether you give up some of your responsibilities, limit the time spent filling various roles, or change the way you perform the related tasks, the important thing is to set some boundaries around your time and energy that will allow you to stay in the profession, remain happy in it, and ultimately be energized enough to serve others. Working harder and harder at your own expense is both shortsighted and reckless. Being a little "selfish" about your boundaries at the outset will enable you to better serve others without the risk of burnout.

Reaching out to Colleagues for Help

The challenge of seeking role clarity is that jobs need to get done and roles do need to be filled. There really is no scenario in which an adult working in a school setting is able to wear one hat and one hat only. All educators have multiple roles to fill, with duties and responsibilities, and people who depend on them to fulfill those obligations.

None of the shifts you identified above can occur in a vacuum. Your actions and beliefs are interwoven with the practices and beliefs of others. Therefore, your "new" thinking cannot be a silent agreement between you and yourself. To have lasting impact on your life and practices, you have to involve others in these changes—especially those with whom you work and live directly.

As you work to define your roles and set reasonable boundaries, try to find some role models. Look around you. Study your immediate colleagues. Who seems most energized in this work? Who seems to be the most resilient? To whom are you most likely to turn when you need a pep talk?

Now, with those people in mind, think about how they seem to balance the various stresses of work. How many roles do they play in the school? How many roles have they chosen *not* to play in the school? Which roles seem to sustain them the most and which roles seem to tax them? How do they move between these roles?

And now one more step: Go and talk to these people! Express your admiration. Share your concerns. Ask questions. At the very least, you and your colleagues can have the self-awareness and humility to admit when you can't perform all of your roles alone, and that you need help. As Roland Barth states in his 1990 book *Improving Schools From Within*, "The relationships among adults in school are the basis, the precondition, the *sine qua non* that allow, energize, and sustain all other attempts at school improvement. Unless adults talk with one another, observe one another, and help one another, very little will change."[6]

You're probably starting to recognize that these chapter topics—support, empowerment, boundaries and expectations—overlap in powerful ways. Educators need to experience support to feel empowered, and they need to be empowered to set reasonable boundaries and expectations.

As McLaughlin and Talbert note in *Professional Communities and the Work of High School Teaching*, teacher-to-teacher trust and relationships are largely based on the building of shared expectations. They also note that the development of relationships is not determined by single events or trainings, but by day-to-day interactions that help create an overall culture of support.[7] As you and your colleagues work to define roles and set boundaries on a personal level, the larger school culture can take on this challenge within the entire workplace.

[*See handout* **3.2** *on CD-ROM*]

PERSONAL INVENTORY

The items below describe frequent themes that arise in Search Institute's staff development trainings with educators. Use these items to reflect on your own experience of boundaries and expectations.

You *set boundaries for yourself:*

	STRONGLY DISAGREE	DISAGREE	NOT SURE	AGREE	STRONGLY AGREE
I have a healthy balance between my work life and my personal life.					
I am able to respect my self-created boundaries without feeling guilty.					
My interests and pursuits outside of school are appreciated and respected by my colleagues.					
I clearly understand what is expected of me at work.					
The amount of my workload is similar to my colleagues' workloads.					
People in my personal life respect the work I do as an educator.					

You *respect the boundaries set by colleagues:*

	STRONGLY DISAGREE	DISAGREE	NOT SURE	AGREE	STRONGLY AGREE
I am comfortable with colleagues setting boundaries that are different from mine.					
I feel that I am a member of a group of professionals who are dedicated to the same mission.					
I voice my concern when I see a colleague in danger of burnout.					

Setting Boundaries at the Administrative Level

The better you and your colleagues can create, name, protect, and share boundaries, the better able you will be to join together in merging your energies toward effective teaching and job satisfaction. But the average reader may be skeptical of this chapter, thinking, "How much control do I have over this situation when my boss continues to ask more of me?" If you are reading and approaching this challenge as an administrator, you can take this conversation to the next level, shaping policies and practices as well as work culture.

Creating sound boundaries and expectations actually serves to ensure that staff can put in extra effort and assume the additional roles necessary to keep a school functioning. In other words, the more defined the boundaries within the structures of the school, the more room available for staff to explore other opportunities for service. Stop to ask yourself these questions:

- Are the school's expectations of staff clear and reasonable?

- Are all members of the staff held to similar expectations?

- Do you and your colleagues share a similar sense of appropriate boundaries between work, life, and collegiality?

- Do you and your colleagues model positive professional conduct?

For example, if staff members are explicitly required within their job descriptions to take on other roles as part of teaching, such as joining curriculum development teams or special education planning teams, that is fine. Staff members may also be required to attend meetings after school on certain days. That is fine, too. But if the requirements keep educators from adequately performing the core duties of teaching, then the conversation around boundaries and expectations needs to address this reality.

The work of a school is never-ending but necessary. The very committees and teams that drain educators' energy might be integral to your school and its success. Therefore, your school's discussion of boundaries and expectations is not entirely about removing work or decreasing involvement. Instead, the conversation is an opportunity for teachers and administrators to come together and figure out roles and workloads that are both reasonable and rewarding for everyone.

How Was *Your* Day at School?

Cora McMichael was 26 years old when she got her master's in education through AmeriCorps and immediately found a job teaching at a public school in New York City. She felt called to the classroom and loved her work. She taught there for three years before moving to Los Angeles. There she found a new teaching job at a progressive and excellent charter school, where she experienced extremely high standards, alternative merit pay, and a general excitement about the challenges of maintaining high goals for all students.

Cora is no longer teaching. What happened?

In both New York and L.A., Cora arrived at work at 6:00 a.m. and stayed until 7:00 p.m. Once she got home, she had hours of grading and planning to do. To reach state and school test standards at her last school (the same tests that would affect her merit pay), Cora was required to give pre-tests and document each student separately. She submitted her lesson plans a full week in advance.

"I had no time, no life," says Cora in reflection. Her husband was the only one she spent any of her free time with. On the weekends, she slept, did laundry, graded, and planned. She made every possible effort to do her best work, and when she took a moment for herself, she felt guilty. This was a cultural norm among the staff in the school. "We had no room for anything else in our lives." School was it. Her colleagues experienced broken relationships and even canceled wedding engagements. Cora estimates that the school loses around 50 percent of its staff each year. She also reports that the school prides itself on running "like a business."

But does it? What business is able to stay profitable while losing that much of its greatest commodity—good employees? What business can remain viable while micromanaging its workforce?

Although this school has taken amazing steps toward providing rigor and relevance for its students, it has also put obstacles in the path of teacher success. The amount of documentation and paperwork required of Cora made it nearly impossible for her to do her job and maintain any quality of life. Time spent with her colleagues, while powerful, was limited. Superiors conducted random, high-pressure classroom observations. Expectations of staff were not always clearly communicated. All of these policies and procedures are within the school's control, and they all push staff toward exhaustion and burnout.

Cora struggles with her decision to leave the profession. Teaching was her identity, and she was really good at it. She didn't want to leave teaching. She wants to get back into it. She *should* be a teacher. But Cora also wants to enjoy her life.

Her experience brings to mind a host of questions: How might her school be as progressive and aggressive in its approach to teacher success as it is to student success? How could the adults in such an intense work culture set boundaries?

Ultimately, Cora's story is a story this book is attempting to rewrite. Her students—and the field of education—lost a great teacher.

Fortunately, the flame of optimism and hope that initially called her to the profession still exists, a flame that will light her way back to the classroom. When she gets there, let's hope she will work with administrators who know how lucky they are and will work hard to keep her.

The Question of Conduct

As you work to set boundaries at the personal level or at the administrative level, remember that these ideas are often promoted through staff conduct. Just as student conduct can make or break the boundaries set in a classroom, staff conduct is essential to promoting boundaries in a school's work climate. Judith Langer, author of the report *Excellence in English in Middle and High School: How Teachers' Professional Lives Support Student Achievement,* contends that a supportive workplace is "shared by administrators, teachers, and students, and lived by actions rather than pronouncements."[8]

For example, if you have explicit rules about the ways in which staff discuss students, that boundary truly manifests itself in a staff-room environment. The topics discussed, the tone of voice, and the appropriateness of comments are lived out in this space much more meaningfully than they are articulated in any handbook. Respect for boundaries (or a lack of respect) is always illuminated by the conduct of staff.

Whether you are struggling to set boundaries for handling parent concerns or balancing duties such as planning lessons and grading papers, staff conduct is the most powerful way to transform boundaries. A shared sense of acceptable conduct will allow a staff to cement its beliefs about the boundaries between what is fair or unfair and what is sustainable or unsustainable.

 [*See handout* **3.3** *on CD-ROM*]

INSTITUTIONAL INVENTORY

Use this checklist to identify the ways that your school is already experiencing healthy boundaries and high expectations among staff.

	STRONGLY DISAGREE	DISAGREE	NOT SURE	AGREE	STRONGLY AGREE
Our work culture supports a healthy balance between professional life and personal life.					
Our staff recognizes the importance of spending social time together.					

	STRONGLY DISAGREE	DISAGREE	NOT SURE	AGREE	STRONGLY AGREE
The school has explicitly defined appropriate conduct and expectations for the adults in the building.					
Most staff adhere to the defined expectations for conduct.					
The energy and time of staff is generally respected.					
The school provides resources and structures that support health and wellness for staff.					
The school does not regularly ask staff to take on too many extra duties beyond teaching responsibilities.					

 [*See handout* **3.4** *on CD-ROM*]

CHAPTER 3:
SHIFTING FROM BURNOUT TO BOUNDARIES

Consider the following shifts as you work to establish boundaries and expectations in your workplace:

BURNING OUT	SETTING HEALTHY BOUNDARIES
I always have to put students' needs first.	If I put my needs first, I'll sustain myself to be a better educator.
If I don't do something, it won't get done at all.	I can actively ask my peers for help to avoid overburdening myself with responsibilities.
I don't have energy left for others in my life after leaving work.	I will protect and save my energy and time in order to remain present in all areas of my life.
I can't give to my work the same way I did earlier in my career.	By choosing my roles carefully and by setting more reasonable boundaries, I will have more energy and enthusiasm for the parts of my job that matter most.
I no longer feel motivated or effective in fulfilling my personal mission in teaching.	I can recognize and enhance the parts of my job that energize me and actively seek solutions to the things that overwhelm me.

Putting Boundaries into Action

You might make some very powerful and personal decisions about your roles as a teacher and what it means to set reasonable boundaries, and these decisions may have a profound effect on you and how you operate in your school. These changes might be noticeable to others. In fact, these changes *should* be noticeable to others. Perhaps the most compelling thing to take away from any discussion about roles and boundaries is that *making this effort could actually change your life.* If you're committed to sustaining yourself in the field of education, surround yourself with fellow educators who are similarly committed to working with you to set and maintain healthy workplace boundaries.

 [*See handout* **3.5** *on CD-ROM*]

NOW WHAT DO I DO?
MOVING IDEAS TO ACTION

Make a pie graph of the roles you fill (teacher, parent, coach, jogger, math team advisor, etc.) It's okay to list "myself" as the role you play when you are engaging in leisure time such as reading, exercising, or watching TV.

Now name one thing you wish you had more time to do:

What role does this desired thing fall under?

To make time for this desired activity and its corresponding role, you will need a larger piece of the pie on the chart you drew above.

Draw a new chart, scaling back one or more other roles to increase your ability to pursue this thing.

Use this visual to guide your personal decision making over the next two weeks. Be mindful of the effect it has on your job satisfaction. Continue to adjust roles until you feel good about the balance you've achieved.

Notes

1. Rudow, B. (1999). Stress and burnout in the teaching profession. In R. Vandenberghe & A. M. Huberman (Eds.), *Understanding and preventing teacher burnout: A sourcebook of international research and practice* (p. 55). Cambridge: Cambridge University Press.

2. Maslach, C. (1982). *Burnout: The cost of caring.* Englewood Cliffs, NJ: Prentice Hall.

3. Cherniss, C. (1980). *Staff burnout: Job stress in the human services.* Beverly Hills, CA: Sage.

4. Farber, B. A. (1991). *Crisis in education: Stress and burnout in the American teacher.* San Francisco: Jossey-Bass.

5. Kahn, R. L., Wolfe, D. M., Quinn, R. P., Shoek, J. D., & Rosenthal, R. A. (1964). *Organizational stress: Studies in role conflict and ambiguity.* New York: Wiley.

6. Barth, R. S. (1990). *Improving schools from within: Teachers, parents, and principals can make a difference.* San Francisco: Jossey-Bass.

7. McLaughlin, M. W. & Talbert, J. E. (2001). *Professional communities and the work of high school teaching.* Chicago: University of Chicago Press.

8. Langer, J. (2000). Excellence in English in middle and high school: How teachers' professional lives support student achievement. *American Educational Research Journal, 37,* 397–439.

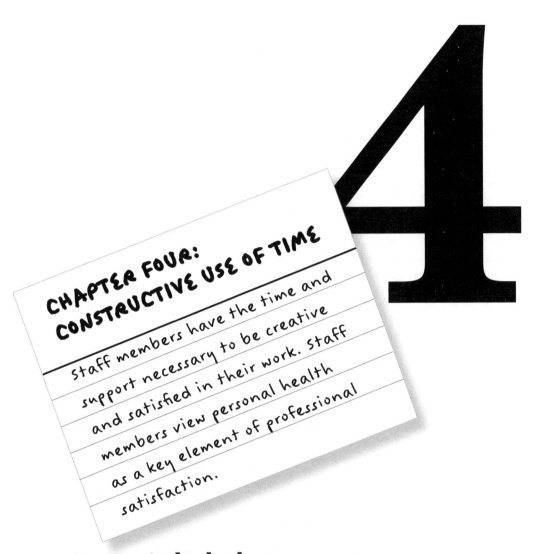

CHAPTER FOUR: CONSTRUCTIVE USE OF TIME

Staff members have the time and support necessary to be creative and satisfied in their work. Staff members view personal health as a key element of professional satisfaction.

I was excited to be there. I loved the class. Ms. Pederson was a fabulous teacher, and my classmates were exceptional. The tone in the room was engaging and invigorating. From the moment we walked into class until the moment we left, we spoke only Spanish. My classmates apparently had no trouble handling this requirement.

I, on the other hand, avoided speaking if I could get away with it. Although it was a great class, when it was time for discussions I would avert my eyes and slink down in my chair. I studied. I tried. I followed most of what I heard and read. But speaking in public was horrible. She would call on me, and sweat would immediately bead on my brow. These episodes went something like this:

Ms. Pederson: Señor Eklund. Qué es (insert rapidly and beautifully spoken Spanish here)?

English translation of my response: "Yes. Pants are good in blue. I like very much the clothes for people to wear in the day."

Slight snickering from my classmates would follow.

I am not recalling a moment in high school or a college course, however. As a teacher, this is how I spent many of my planning periods for a semester. Wishing to relearn Spanish and wanting to watch one of my favorite colleagues teach, I asked Marilyn Pederson if I could sit in on her AP Spanish class. I would do the homework, study for the quizzes, and, yes, respond when called on.

While occasionally embarrassing and clearly quite humbling, I cannot think of time better spent during my planning hours. In addition to reacquainting myself with my long-lost Spanish skills, I also reaped a host of benefits that were instrumental to my own personal and professional development. This is what constructive use of time is all about.

questions
TO CONSIDER

- **Does your** professional involvement **with the school enhance your quality of life?**

- **Do you enjoy the** cultural, generational, and societal variety **that a school setting provides you?**

- **Do you utilize** school resources **in your own interests and pursuits?**

- **Are you able to use time and relationships with students and colleagues to engage in** creative activities **that enhance your personal health and wellness?**

Defining "Constructive"

There are a couple of common pitfalls when it comes to using the word "constructive" in this context. The first is the assumption that it means "productive." Certainly teachers who use their time constructively *are* productive, but this chapter has more to do with finding a balance between work and play, between core responsibilities and chosen interests. Just as Chapter 3 invited you to focus on balance within your work, this chapter invites you to find a balance between your job and your "extracurricular" pursuits.

Although this category describes efforts that might traditionally be termed "extracurricular" or "cocurricular," it's important to note that this is not simply a call for recreation or relaxation. Certainly there is an energizing quality to achieving this balance between business and pleasure, but it is important to recognize that discovering this balance is not frivolous. This is about finding meaningful outlets for your creativity, acquiring new skills, and making the time to feel satisfied and challenged in your professional life.

Making Time and Taking Time

You may be fortunate enough to work in a school that makes superb decisions about how to give time to teachers so they can do their best work. Careful scheduling, joint planning hours, sufficient preparation periods, and thoughtful use of professional development hours are all critical to protecting the time of educators. But those protections will only go so far. At some point, time management becomes a personal issue.

There is a fallacy in our concept of time that sets up a mental block when we try to find a healthier balance in work commitments. We often phrase our stress with the words, "I know I should do _____, but I don't have the time." This sentence reflects the enormity of our mental to-do list. While it's true that there are significant demands on our time, always resigning ourselves to this notion is defeating and potentially self-destructive.

Our language when discussing time is far too passive in that respect. We wearily throw out the suggestion that *if* we had time, then we'd seek new opportunities and take care of ourselves. Leaving time to chance—hoping to *find* the time—is the same as admitting that we are not going to actively *make* the time for the things that truly enrich our professional lives. If we morph the original sentence to reflect a more hopeful, proactive mindset, we might instead say, "I know I need to _____, so I am going to make the time to do it."

The problem for an educator is that time doesn't feel entirely like a personal matter. A teacher's time doesn't belong solely to the teacher—it really *does* belong to the students. But if we believe this too fully, we are at serious risk for burnout. If we think that being an educator means *always* "being there" for students at the expense of our own needs, then it's no surprise that we feel guilty when we make efforts to reclaim time for ourselves.

This guilt can evoke some challenging imagery when we think about taking time back for our own self-preservation. We may imagine a stack of papers left on a desk, ungraded and locked away for the night. We might picture an office door closed during some of the hours when it was once open, or as a classroom closed up for the evening earlier than in the past. Interpreted on a very basic level, preserving time for ourselves means taking something back that we once willingly gave freely to others.

Frankly, when I took that Spanish class, I really couldn't afford to give up those planning hours. Sitting in that class certainly took away some of that precious time I had to meet with students, plan lessons, and grade and organize papers. But in the long run, I found that I couldn't afford *not* to take the time. The sense of release and variety that came with taking the time to do this fed my spirit and energy in a way that far outweighed any consequences. Ultimately, my students benefited as much as I did.

The Opportunities That Surround You

Basically, the thrust of this chapter is to create a sense of reinvention about what a school life can look like. I think of my own experience working in a high school. My career there gave me a social life (supportive, like-minded colleagues), a gym membership (using school facilities), cultural opportunities (concerts and plays), and free entertainment (games and events)—not to mention a valuable roster of world-class babysitters for my children! As I worked hard to create distinct boundaries between my work and personal life, I also began to see ways that my work life could enrich my personal life.

Schools provide access to an experience that few people get to enjoy in a workplace. The cultural and generational diversity within a school community is quite remarkable. The backgrounds and traditions of your student body and staff provide countless opportunities to participate with and learn from a variety of people. Teachers also have a rare window into the lives and perspectives of a younger generation. Learning from your students about their interests and skills is not only a key part of building relationships with students, but also gives you exposure to a worldview and understanding that most adults lack.

In part, this conversation is about how you benefit from the school, not just how the school benefits from you. Too often we adopt a stance that is entirely one-sided: What can I do for this school? By doing so, we overlook the notion that by engaging with the school differently and using our time differently, we too can be recipients of all that a school has to offer. Ask yourself these questions:

- What school resource that you presently don't use could benefit you personally or professionally?

- What after-school activity might you personally benefit from but presently do not schedule in your life?

A school community is a resource that is almost unlimited in its potential to enrich your life. Participating in the activities of a wide variety of adult and student groups—everything from chess club to improvisational theater—are all opportunities to interact and stretch yourself beyond what you might normally experience. While the financial perks of teaching might be few, the benefits of how you use your time with the school can be tremendous.

Managing Time on a Personal Level

Of course, having a rich and balanced life isn't just about connecting with the school itself. It's about making your time your own, and that has little to do with your school or colleagues. The logical foundation of this conversation is something we all know to be true: **the happier and healthier we are away from work, the happier and healthier we'll be while at work.** This happiness is about individual health, relationships, pursuit of personal interests, and maintaining time for all of the above.

To truly take control of our time, we need to reframe our view of our work and the value of our time. Think about the way you currently spend your "free time," and ask yourself the following questions:

- If you dedicated one planning hour a week to doing something for your own personal and professional benefit besides classroom tasks, what would you *choose* to do with that time?

- If you dedicated one evening a week to doing something for your own personal and professional benefit besides school duties, what would you *choose* to do with that evening?

Notice that both of these questions imply that you need to give up one thing in order to gain another. A planning hour usually spent in one fashion is going to be rededicated toward another gain. This is all part of the attitude you need to adopt if you are going to guard your time for the things that energize you.

As an exercise, plan out a week of your teaching in which you schedule not only your lessons and prior commitments, but also your free time (including your planning hours). Before this time collapses in on itself, schedule your own needs into the available time. See if you can balance your work and commitments with time for socializing and engaging in other activities. If you are not in the habit of scheduling time for the things you want to accomplish personally, get in the habit. If the things you care about are not protected within your schedule, they are too likely to go away. You need to schedule your own time in a manner that creates space for you to sustain your energy and pursue your interests. Try this for a month.

At the end of the month, assess the impact this has had on your professional performance and personal energy. How did scheduling time for yourself affect your attitude about work? About students? About colleagues? When you value your time fully and find a balance that feels right, this is a tremendous boost to your strength as an educator.

Whether you pursue your interests at school in the available time during and after school hours, or seek outside opportunities for growth through other classes or activities, the point is to make time for the things that refresh, challenge, and energize you. Use the personal inventory below to get started.

 [*See handout* **4.1** *on CD-ROM*]

PERSONAL INVENTORY

The items below describe frequent themes that arise in Search Institute's staff development trainings with educators. Use these items to reflect on your own time commitments.

You have *balanced time commitments:*

	STRONGLY DISAGREE	DISAGREE	NOT SURE	AGREE	STRONGLY AGREE
I spend enough time with my family and friends to make me feel energized.					
I make time to pursue my own interests and passions.					
I have time during each workday to spend with other adults.					
I practice self-restraint in order to not become over-extended.					
I take time to engage in my own learning and professional development.					
I get enough sleep to sustain my energy at work and in life.					

You *encourage colleagues to have balanced time commitments:*

	STRONGLY DISAGREE	DISAGREE	NOT SURE	AGREE	STRONGLY AGREE
I pitch in and help when my colleagues are feeling over-worked.					
I encourage colleagues to practice behaviors of wellness.					
I intervene if a colleague is overworked or stressed.					
I share with my colleagues an overall sense of the role that work will play in our lives.					

Valuing Staff Time at the Institutional Level

A key ingredient to ensuring that staff members experience constructive use of time is to make it a schoolwide priority. It's important to open up this discussion with the entire staff because the more effectively colleagues are supported in this effort, the more likely it is that they will use their time to recharge and pursue the interests that renew them. As staff members work on personal growth in this area,

How Was *Your* Day at School?

Scott Butler was a counselor at Millard West High School in Millard, Nebraska, for 12 years. Like many schools' cultures, his workplace seemed to have an unspoken competition among the adults: Who works the hardest? Who can come to work the earliest? Who can stay the latest?

Scott figured there had to be a better way. He made a pact with his colleague, Susan: They both had families waiting at home for them, so they agreed to leave the building at a decent time. They chose 4:30. Each day at 4:30, one would show up at the other's office and they would wrap up the day.

But what about the days when their desks were piled high, and leaving just wasn't possible? On those days, they reminded each other of their priorities: No matter what, the work would still be there in the morning—but at that moment, their families were waiting for them. Often one of them would stand in the other's doorway, waiting for the completion of one last task, but then it was time to leave.

They shut off their computers. They put on their jackets. And they made the long stroll out to the parking lot. They often spent ten or fifteen minutes talking about the day, their work, or life in general. After this brief dose of collegiality, they got in their cars and went home. In addition to feeling better about their work, they both reported feeling like better parents and spouses.

This is a simple effort, but it transformed the work experience of these two colleagues. They supported each other, empowered each other, created shared boundaries, and ultimately made the most of their time—personally and professionally.

you can begin to foster a work climate that says, "We are working together toward the benefit of others and ourselves, while we individually continue to grow and develop as humans." In doing so, you will ultimately create a group of adults who respect each other's time and value the hours they spend together.

One way to get the ball rolling is to initiate these conversations during professional development or some other kind of staff training. Use the opportunity to discuss how people feel about the ways they use their time. What do they consider a waste of time? What do they consider time well spent? Explore the group's assumptions, and debate which attitudes promote the constructive use of time and which attitudes inhibit it. Once you have a shared sense of values and direction with your colleagues, you will also have a better idea of how to support each other's choices about how you spend your time.

If it's true that collegiality is one of the leading factors in job satisfaction, then spending time with colleagues needs to become a larger priority. If it's true that health and wellness are integral to job performance, then committing time to this facet of staff development is imperative. Use the institutional inventory below to assess the opportunities your school has to improve these efforts.

 [*See handout* **4.2** *on CD-ROM*]

INSTITUTIONAL INVENTORY

Use this checklist to identify the ways that your school is already experiencing balanced time commitments among staff.

	STRONGLY DISAGREE	DISAGREE	NOT SURE	AGREE	STRONGLY AGREE
Our school sets reasonable expectations for time spent doing work outside of school hours.					
Our school accepts staff members saying "no" to requests if they need to balance their time differently.					

continued

	STRONGLY DISAGREE	DISAGREE	NOT SURE	AGREE	STRONGLY AGREE
Our school regularly provides opportunities for staff to have unstructured time with one another.					
The amount of time spent in scheduled meetings is reasonable and fair to staff.					

 [See handout **4.3** *on CD-ROM]*

CHAPTER 4: SHIFTING FROM OVEREXTENDED TO A HEALTHY BALANCE

Consider the following shifts as you work to foster the constructive use of time in your workplace:

WORK *ALWAYS* COMES FIRST	BALANCED TIME COMMITMENTS
Taking time to pursue my own interests and passions will negatively affect my work performance.	Being engaged in my own pursuits will not only fulfill me personally but will also equip me to be a better educator.
I can't take time for myself during the day because there is always too much to do.	Even if I work every minute of every day, there will still be work to do. Therefore, seeking daily opportunities to sustain and increase my energy and enthusiasm will help me more joyfully fulfill the challenges of teaching.
My own needs are in conflict with the duties of teaching.	Not paying attention to my own needs will only lead to exhaustion, stress, and sadness.
I need to work as hard or harder than everyone around me.	I need to work at a level that not only supports the work of the school but also respects my own limitations.
Conversation or social time with colleagues is a waste of time.	Positive relationships with other adults are a key element of my work satisfaction.
If I don't look as tired and stressed as other teachers, I won't look like I'm doing my job.	I need to set reasonable and healthy ways of measuring my effort and worth.

Putting Constructive Use of Time into Action

Returning to the story that opened this chapter, it's helpful to remember that, despite the way it sounds, "constructive use of time" is neither about relaxation nor productivity. It's about self-improvement. It's about finding the time—making the time—for educators to grow and challenge themselves in ways that are energizing rather than draining.

When I took that Spanish class, I had the opportunity to remind myself what it felt like to be a student: The stress of cramming for vocabulary quizzes. The joy of doing well. The value of receiving encouragement from a teacher when I was struggling. The panic of being called on to speak in front of others. These reminders transformed my understanding of the role I was playing in my own students' lives and learning. Above all, I learned that the best trait I could show my students wasn't necessarily authoritative brilliance in my own content area, but a genuine curiosity about and desire for new knowledge.

It is fitting that Constructive Use of Time is the final "external" category in this book. Ultimately, using your time more thoughtfully and intentionally will influence all of the external factors you are working to address. As you shift your thinking to the "internal" chapters in Part II, the decision to balance your commitments carefully will give you the time you need to reevaluate your values and your identity as an educator.

 [*See handout* **4.4** *on CD-ROM*]

NOW WHAT DO I DO?
MOVING IDEAS TO ACTION

1. Identify one personal activity (e.g., riding a bike, reading for pleasure, fishing) that increases your energy:

2. Identify one professional activity (e.g., talking with colleagues, limiting office hours, reading educational journals) that increases your energy:

3. Identify one use of your professional time that drains your energy (e.g., attending multiple weekly committee meetings or grading homework through the lunch hour):

4. Identify one way you could use this same time in a way that rejuvenates you (e.g., going for a walk or eating lunch with a colleague):

For the next two weeks, make the changes you've described above, making time for the things that sustain you and eliminating or reducing the practices that drain you. Pay attention to the impact these changes have on your performance as an educator.

5. Which of these efforts had the most positive effect on your job satisfaction? Why or why not?

6. Did any of these changes impair the quality of your work? Why or why not?

7. Do you feel guilty when you make different choices with your time? Why or why not?

8. Of all the things you've tried, which new behavior or activity benefits both your job performance and your job satisfaction the most? Commit to making this a permanent change in your life.

Find a "time partner": someone who will help you sustain this commitment to your improved job satisfaction. Ask your time partner to encourage, challenge, and remind you as necessary about the importance of this effort.

Part II:

IDENTIFYING AND BUILDING INTERNAL ASSETS — THE VALUES, SKILLS, AND BELIEFS NECESSARY TO FULLY ENGAGE WITH OTHER COLLEAGUES AND TO FUNCTION WELL IN THE WORKPLACE.

As you shift your focus from work conditions to the internal asset categories of healthy teacher development, consider the following analogy: The bus is packed. The students are in their seats. You're off for an elaborate weekend field trip of camping in the mountains. You're driving the bus, and as you near the base of the mountains and head into dense forests, you notice that the fuel light is on. You're just passing by the last service station for several miles. But the kids are so excited to get going! Stopping now will delay their fun. So you head onward. And run out of gas. And the trip is ruined.

Unless you are taking care of yourself as an educator, your students will suffer. In the analogy of the bus trip, the insanity involved in not stopping to refuel is instantly apparent: Why would anyone invite the dread of hearing the motor die and dealing with the subsequent whining and panic involved in being stranded? As a reader, it's easy to anticipate the obvious consequences of heading into the hills while running on empty.

As you take stock of your own "gas tank," consider the following questions:

- What are warning signs that you're running low on fuel?

- How often do you drive until the warning light comes on?

- How many of your colleagues appear to have depleted their fuel tanks? Which colleagues appear to keep their tanks reasonably full?

- How do you refuel? Who helps you do this professionally?

- How might colleagues carpool or share driving responsibilities in order to avoid falling asleep at the wheel?

 [*See handout* **PART 2** *on CD-ROM*]

It is encouraging to note that these questions do not advocate a solely "do-it-yourself" mentality. On the contrary, these questions reveal the many ways you can reach out to colleagues, supervisors, and mentors to help you plan for a successful trip.

This analogy offers a simple but powerful caution: without proper care and concern for your "fuel light," your students will ultimately pay the price. An attempt to serve the students and their needs and desires without paying attention to the limitations and stresses connected to those demands will inevitably result in consequences that are damaging for you *and* the students.

Just as a flight attendant reminds you to put on your own oxygen mask before assisting others, this section reminds you how dangerous it is to neglect your own needs "for the good of the students"—because filling your gas tank *is* good for the students.

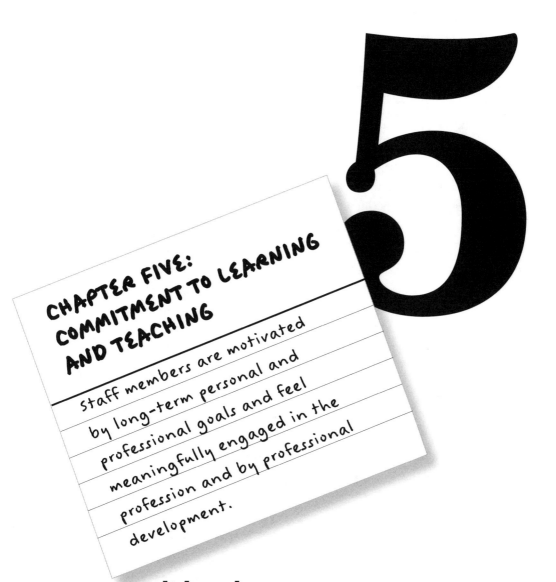

5

CHAPTER FIVE: COMMITMENT TO LEARNING AND TEACHING

Staff members are motivated by long-term personal and professional goals and feel meaningfully engaged in the profession and by professional development.

As an English teacher, I was able to teach a wide array of courses. At one point I had the privilege of team-teaching Cultural Anthropology—a course that changed me forever. This experience reminded me daily of how much I could learn from a fellow teacher.

I taught with David Herring, my good friend and the chair of the social studies department. If the truth be told, we piloted the course before either of us had any true background in cultural anthropology. We carried the "you're always 24 hours ahead of the kids" mantra to its furthest limits in the first year of the course. But because we had each other, we were able to learn along the way, immersing ourselves in study in a fashion that we wouldn't have been able to do separately. On many days I simply sat in the auditorium with the students, learning from the lesson Dave had prepared for that day. It was in that setting that I rediscovered my own love of learning. It was also where I cemented my love of teaching, teachers, and knowledge itself. My experience in that class renewed my commitment to the profession of education.

Each year we meet new groups of students ready to progress in and master the skills we teach in our classes. And then each year we see them leave, only to have new groups enter our classes the next year. Watching that annual progress is the magic of teaching; however, the repetitive nature of the work can be taxing. How can we shift from being just vessels of information toward being lifelong learners— co-learners with colleagues and students? Doing so gives us renewed interest in and enthusiasm toward our work and allows us to avoid stagnation. It is almost impossible to overstate the importance of commitment in the work of educators. Without long-term goals supported by consistent and rigorous effort, complacency can creep into our work, threatening our ability to stay fresh and fulfilled. One key ingredient to commitment is an ability to set and strive toward goals. The personal and professional goals we set for ourselves can be the impetus for self-improvement and can motivate us to seek help from others. Even more importantly, our goals allow us to set and reach benchmarks along the path of teaching that provide moments of celebration and a sense of progress.

This chapter will help you explore what it means to be committed to your profession. As you gain a richer understanding of the things that keep you engaged in your work, you are better equipped to set and pursue personal and professional goals. By clearly defining and marking your progress toward these goals, you will experience a more fulfilling sense of momentum and accomplishment.

questions
TO CONSIDER

o **What motivates you to be a** better teacher?

o **What professional goals help you stay** committed to learning and teaching?

o **Which professional goals are you presently** working toward?

o **How do your goals inform your** daily practice and attitude?

Becoming a "Master Teacher"

As with any profession, there is an art and a science to teaching. Separating the art from the science can be instrumental in helping you gain a broader perspective on your profession. Thinking about the qualities listed in the table below, imagine the strengths and weaknesses different teachers bring to the profession, both individually and collectively within a school:

SCIENCE OF TEACHING	ART OF TEACHING
• Classroom management strategies	• Handling students who are in crisis
• Application of technology	• Adjusting instruction for temporary distractions
• Acquisition of core content	• Communicating with parents
• Instructing toward desired testing outcomes	• Being good to others despite fatigue and stress
• Use of variety of instructional approaches	• Establishing respectful relationships with students
• Providing for varied learning styles	• Creating an inviting classroom environment

Reading through this list of teaching characteristics, you can see that it's going to take something beyond workshops, higher degrees, and textbooks to truly achieve the status of "master teacher." Too often professional development focuses solely on the items listed in the first column, the science of teaching. But what happens when we redefine "master teacher" to include the art of the profession? This teacher would possess the power of content mastery and pedagogy, and also the human and relational skills that mark the very best of the teaching profession.

The whole concept of master teachers is most powerful when individuals begin to seek knowledge and relationships with other master teachers in the staff. This can lead to many conversations that start with something like, "I know we don't teach the same subject, but I was wondering . . ." Perhaps even, "We hardly know each other, but I've noticed that . . ."

Every teacher develops a unique bag of tricks. While one teacher might have a knack for reaching the students with whom everyone else on staff seems to struggle, another teacher seems particularly adept at teaching the "gifted and talented" kids. While one teacher is amazing at eliciting student participation, another teacher is skilled at connecting with adults. What happens when these experts get together? Everyone is good at something. Everyone needs to improve on something. All teachers have kids who love them. All teachers have kids who do not. This is why a staff of combined talents works, and this is why staff members need each other.

Becoming a master teacher cannot happen in isolation, and it cannot happen without a sincere desire to learn and grow. We know that one of the best ways for our students to learn is to get *them* to teach. The relationship between learning and teaching is well documented with young people. The act of teaching energizes their thinking and crystallizes their understanding of a given concept. A similar symbiotic relationship exists between an educator's experience of learning and teaching. **The more you embrace your role as a learner, constantly striving to improve in your knowledge and skills, the more you will succeed as a teacher.**

In a Search Institute–led focus group of educators at a Minneapolis public high school, teachers were asked, "What keeps you motivated as an educator?"

One English teacher replied, "After 25 years, I still don't get it. What is teaching? How do I do it well? I still don't fully understand this job."

What's striking about his comment isn't what he said, but that he was able to articulate his own limitations and need for growth. This humility and earnest sense of wonderment is not a weakness; rather, it is the hallmark of an educator engaged in an ongoing self-improvement that transcends practice and pedagogy and is centered in a deeper exploration of what it means to learn and teach. With that attitude, his classroom must be a place of frank conversation and communal inquiry. Put simply, he is as committed to *learning* as he is to *teaching*.

If this notion took root in professional development circles, imagine the tremendous gains made among staff as they openly and readily relied on each other's expertise and wisdom. This job is hard enough without having to create the perception that individually we know everything already! The longer we teach, the more we discover how much we don't know.

Above all, committing to lifelong learning is simply one of the most powerful acts of modeling that teachers can provide to students. Satisfying our own curiosities and questions shows young people the finest traits of what it should mean to be a student. Our own pursuit of knowledge shows young people a passion for learning, the humility that comes with never ending our search for enlightenment, and the joyful effort that comes with seeking wisdom and truth. We would be remiss if our students entered our classrooms simply to download facts, figures, and words from our mouths to their brains, with little real scholarship occurring. How powerful then to show them what learning for learning's sake can look like.

What It Means to Be Engaged

After exploring the internal commitment to learning and teaching, it's also important to explore what it means to be meaningfully engaged in the profession—the second component of this asset category. The phrase "meaningfully engaged" implies a sense of purpose. Of course, to an educator, this goes without saying. Teaching is not a job where simply "showing up" is the equivalent of actually performing the job. Teaching isn't only about being in the classroom or going through rote tasks. Instead, teaching is something that requires a sense of purpose and dedication that relies on an even broader sense of meaning and value. Take away "meaningful engagement" and it's difficult to imagine that much commitment to teaching remains.

You know this to be true from your own experiences in the classroom. You know that when you feel connected to what you're doing and with your colleagues, you're both more successful and more joyful in the work itself. You know that an engaged, committed educator in the classroom is central to the success of students. And you know that your own commitment and engagement is central to *your* success.

This section will guide you through an exploration of your own engagement to your work. The questions that follow will assist you in identifying some of the key elements of your attachment to the profession of teaching.

Are You Engaged in Your Work?

- How much do you enjoy your time with students?

- To what degree do you feel your teaching makes a difference in the lives of your students?

- To what degree do you feel your teaching makes an impact on the broader community in which you teach?

- How connected do you feel to teachers in your building and to the field of education?

- How satisfying is your present career progression?

Your answers to these questions serve as a strong indicator of how you view your work. If you discover some areas where you are presently disengaged, it is important to think about how you could increase your sense of connection in those areas.

For example, if you find that you are struggling to enjoy your time with students, which can be utterly debilitating for an educator, it's time to step back and try to understand why. Here are only a few of the questions you could consider as you work toward trying to reconnect with your students:

- Which responsibilities or attitudes have prevented you from giving the time and energy you'd like to give to your students? How could those same tasks be performed differently, or how could you adjust your attitude toward the role these tasks play in your classroom?

- Have the pressures of the various roles you've accepted left you without the time and energy you'd like to devote toward your students? If so, how could you regain those things?

- Has a negative relationship with an individual student or group of students soured your view of all your students? If so, how can you mend your relationships with these difficult students in order to retain your energy for the other students?

This action-oriented thinking allows you to either reengage with students or engage with them in a new way. Most likely, these new connections will remind you why you chose to teach in the first place.

Setting Goals to Sustain Commitment

Now that you've explored what it means to be meaningfully engaged and committed to learning and teaching, how do you make these concepts real in your life as an educator? The goals you set, and the impact these goals have on your ongoing practice, are central to your teaching career. Your goals and your drive to reach these goals can be described as *achievement motivation*. Here are a few ways you might think about whether or not you experience it:

- You have clear goals for your professional development.

- You have incentives and reasons to improve and progress.

- You feel motivated by the general goal of becoming a "master teacher."

- You can identify small steps toward reaching larger goals.

Achievement motivation means that you have clear and explicit professional goals for your own continuing development. The power of these (and all) goals comes from the relationship between the goal itself and your perception of your own potential. The more directly your goals are related to your strengths and weaknesses, the more your journey toward these outcomes will sustain your passions and energies.

Also, it's imperative that you state these goals in a detailed and clear fashion that allows you to measure your own progress. It is one thing to say, "This year I will be a better teacher." It's another to say, "This year I will work on my ability to ask critical questions of students." One presents a vague, global goal. The other offers something one could work toward and monitor. You'll have a stronger sense of accomplishment if you establish the latter.

As you start evaluating your goals, the metaphor of diet and exercise can be helpful. "Losing weight" may seem like a measurable goal, but deciding how many pounds to lose does not help you identify the necessary steps to lose the pounds. Goals that focus on specific dietary and exercise behaviors are much easier to accomplish. If you say, "I will walk an extra 10 minutes every day," or, "I will eat an extra serving of fruits or vegetables for lunch each day," you've identified a concrete step toward the larger goal. Similarly, as you reflect on your teaching and sense of fulfillment and happiness, try to identify present obstacles and challenges that are in your way and create goals that are targeted at those needs.

Once you have begun to isolate some of these areas for potential growth and improvement, then it's also time to identify the resources and colleagues you'll need to achieve the goals. Done in isolation, many of your goals will sputter out. Once you've identified your areas of focus, you should also identify which colleagues can help you achieve your goals. In fact, your own goal setting can be an act of collegiality.

Some of the goals you and your colleagues tackle may be quite mundane. Perhaps a portion of the curriculum remains vexing or underutilized. Perhaps a school policy has impeded your work. **Countless goals, both big and small, can all serve the same macro-goal: to become better at, and get more joy from, your work.**

What we're describing here is a strong personal and internal commitment to progress. To rely on external rewards alone or to seek only external incentives would do little to provide you with the necessary support to sustain your work.

Therefore, one of the central, internal reasons to improve is that the more competent you are at your job and the better you *feel* about doing your job, the happier you're going to be doing the work. Teaching can shake your confidence on a daily basis—even more so if you have self-doubts. Therefore, a primary reason for setting concrete goals is to increase your own personal satisfaction. Essentially you're giving yourself reasons to celebrate your commitment to the profession. Consider the following as you set goals for yourself:

- What are the specific elements of teaching that bring you the most joy?

- What are the specific elements of teaching that cause you the most frustration, exhaustion, or sadness?

- What specific goals could you set to encourage the positive parts of your work?

- What specific goals could you set to remove impediments to your enjoyment of this work?

- What rewards could you give yourself for the successful completion of these goals?

All goal setting should be done so that you are both better at your job and more joyful in it. Your effectiveness and happiness are intertwined and need your thoughtful, daily, and consistent attention. None of this line of questioning should conflict with the goals that are set *for* you, of course. District initiatives and department goals can all be met within the more general environment of your own professional progress. In fact, many of your own goals might be set in such a way as to support or better deal with external goals as you practice the art and science of teaching in your own classroom. When teachers, administrators, and other school staff work together, their individual goals form a network of commitment throughout the entire school community.

The Problem of Delayed Happiness

When it comes to feeling committed and setting goals in the profession of teaching, educators face a strangely inverted adjustment period as they enter the workforce. In most careers there is a "honeymoon" period, characterized by hopeful excitement about the unknown. The energy of new challenges sustains workers for a time, only to be replaced by the potential stress, boredom, and daily demands of work. Certainly teaching can feel this way, but teachers often experience the opposite phenomenon: Most new teachers are told *not* to judge the profession for a period of time—usually a minimum of three years. New teachers are told to "hang in there" for multiple years until they are able to at long last enjoy their work. But three years is a long time! It's a dismal prospect to enter a career in which you are immediately discouraged from enjoying your work for months and months until you finally crack the code.

This whole line of thinking is even more upsetting if you've been teaching for longer than three years and still don't feel satisfied. How long are you willing to wait for professional happiness? At the risk of asking a strange question, wouldn't you be happier now if you were happier *now*?

It does take time to become good at teaching; as in other professions, experience brings skill development. All educators can recall the challenges that accompany inexperience. However, the challenges do not go away. Teaching might become *easier*, but it will never be *easy*. What is it then that can sustain educators throughout all stages of a career? This is where the commitment levels of individual teachers become crucial to the larger organization. This commitment is at the core of the long-term sustainability of teaching careers.

Of course there are tangible, quantifiable ways to create professional growth plans that lead to improvements in theory and practice. These are critical to the ongoing professional development that is central to becoming a master teacher.

For the most part, these types of measurement play out on the most literal and observable of planes: educators can identify what they've learned and how that learning manifests itself in their classroom practice. These goals are grounded in pedagogy, application of classroom resources, and implementation of new technologies. All of these elements of professional development are intrinsic to progress.

But teachers also need to be allowed to measure accomplishments not only in terms of "What concrete outcomes did my students achieve?" but also, "How did I improve as a teacher?" This learning might very well be separate from the content of the educator's classroom instruction.

Once again, it's helpful to examine the advice we give our students. We stress that school is more than grades and tests. We stress that students need to possess a love of learning—the type of learning that comes from good discussion, reading for pleasure, involvement in clubs or activities, and following personal intellectual passions and curiosities. We love to see our students passionately in search of knowledge, which we hope turns into wisdom as they age. Likewise, if educators wish to foster a deeper commitment to *teaching*, we need to facilitate and honor teachers who retain their commitment to *learning* and are constantly improving in their work. The alternative is the sort of lifeless learning we fear our students will practice.

 [*See handout* **5.1** *on CD-ROM*]

PERSONAL INVENTORY

The items below describe frequent themes that arise in Search Institute's staff development trainings with educators. Use these items to reflect on your own experience of commitment to learning and teaching.

You *feel committed to learning and teaching:*

	STRONGLY DISAGREE	DISAGREE	NOT SURE	AGREE	STRONGLY AGREE
I care deeply about giving my students a high-quality education.					
I know my professional strengths and weaknesses.					
I am not intimidated by admitting areas for growth.					
I feel that I am continually improving as an educator.					
I can name concrete goals I've set for myself as an educator.					
The opportunities I'm given for professional development directly affect my performance and my enjoyment of the work of education.					
I set personal goals apart from work that influence my use of time and allotment of energy.					
I am committed to the broader goals of education and, through it, creating a better world.					
I enjoy learning from my colleagues.					
I am intellectually challenged and provoked by the profession and my peers.					

You *foster your colleagues' commitment to learning and teaching:*

	STRONGLY DISAGREE	DISAGREE	NOT SURE	AGREE	STRONGLY AGREE
I try to help my colleagues seek opportunities to learn new things.					
I offer my colleagues opportunities to discuss meaningful education-focused topics.					
I invite colleagues into my classroom.					

continued

	STRONGLY DISAGREE	DISAGREE	NOT SURE	AGREE	STRONGLY AGREE
I ask colleagues meaningful questions about teaching and students.					
I share resources with my colleagues.					

Strengthening Commitment at the Institutional Level

Much of this discussion is obviously tied to the school as a larger organization and the way it both supports individual commitment and celebrates accomplishments. Just as schools support and congratulate students for their commitment to learning and academic achievement, schools must show that they value the goals and accomplishments of teachers and other staff.

A growing trend in the education world is tying teacher salaries to professional development and goal setting. Most of the best-informed alternative pay structures recognize salary growth as an essential piece to an individual's personal growth. This is one of the clearest links between goals and incentives. While there are many differing opinions about and approaches to this trend, it's worth recognizing the power incentives can have in sustaining a teacher's career.

Incentive pay that is tied to professional goals really has a two-fold benefit: increased salaries for educators *and* systemic support for professional goals. One can imagine that teachers in this setting experience a positive change in the conversations they're having with other staff members and an increased sense of empowerment as they strive to attain their own goals. One should note, however, that salaries alone only go so far in retaining quality educators. According to a study in a partnership between the Center for Teacher Quality and the California Department of Education, "Better compensation matters to teachers, but unless their classroom and school environment is conducive to good teaching, better compensation is not likely to improve teacher retention rates."[1]

While commitment is a highly personal experience, it is important that the goals of educators play out within an environment that recognizes, supports, and celebrates their work toward these goals. Use the institutional inventory on page 100 to identify your school's opportunities to strengthen these efforts.

How Was *Your* Day at School?

In her first year as a middle school educator, Ann* was nurtured, protected, connected, and encouraged. Her administrator was mindful of all staff members' needs and temperaments. When things were stressful, the staff took time to loosen up and relax, even holding a staff marshmallow battle one day after school. Colleagues worked and talked with one another, and Ann was thoughtfully and personally guided through her first year of teaching. In this setting, Ann was ready to commit to a lifelong career in teaching.

Then her position was cut, and she was forced to switch schools.

Ann's second school was like a case study in what it means to have a caustic staff climate: an overwhelming workload, unstated expectations (followed by unexpected punishment), rumors, and sabotage made for a miserable experience. Even when she wrote grants and took on leadership roles, she found herself ostracized by others on her team, a recipient of suspicion rather than recognition. Although Ann remained devoted to her students and her classroom, she was no longer thriving as an educator but merely surviving.

By the end of her second year of teaching, Ann's friends and family were throwing her a party simply because she had made it through the year. Instead of celebrating her excellence as an educator, they were celebrating her ability to withstand the toxic conditions.

What does Ann have to say about all of this? "I would leave the profession of teaching before I went back to that school."

Does it really need to be this way?

When a culture of mistrust and anger pervades a school, it is difficult for educators to keep sight of their commitment to learning and teaching. What would happen in Ann's second school if the adults collectively pushed the pause button and said, "Wait a minute! We're not happy. This isn't working. We can do better than this"?

The good news is that schools can change from within. By nurturing collegiality, professional development, and individual goal setting, the field of education can retain great teachers like Ann.

Names have been omitted or changed for the sake of anonymity.

 [*See handout* **5.2** *on CD-ROM*]

INSTITUTIONAL INVENTORY

Use this checklist to identify the ways that your school already experiences a strong commitment to learning and teaching among staff.

	STRONGLY DISAGREE	DISAGREE	NOT SURE	AGREE	STRONGLY AGREE
Our staff members are committed to learning new things and growing professionally.					
There is a clear environment of intellectual stimulation among staff.					
Staff are given time to engage in conversations about education and current affairs.					
Learning is an intrinsic part of our staff development time.					
Debate and discourse are encouraged in a respectful manner among staff.					
Our school offers tangible incentives for teachers who work hard to improve in the profession.					
Our staff members have a shared sense of commitment and a work climate that supports their individual goals.					

CHAPTER 5:
SHIFTING FROM BURDENED TO COMMITTED

Consider the following shifts as you work to build a commitment to learning and teaching in your workplace:

TEACHING IS A BURDEN	TEACHING IS A FULFILLING CHALLENGE
I hope I can get by and survive my days of teaching.	I need to seek opportunities and relationships that allow me to thrive in this profession.
Between students, parents, and colleagues, I have no room in this profession for myself.	The quality of the relationships I have with others will be dependent on how healthy and happy I am.
Because of all of the external pressures placed on me, I can't teach the way that I want to.	No amount of external pressure can take over my own attitude and behaviors toward teaching.
My work saps me of the best parts of myself, leaving little left to offer others.	With the support of other adults in the school, I can sustain my own energy and spirit so that work actually increases my ability to be present with others.

Putting Commitment into Action

Ultimately, personal commitment to improving as an educator, colleague, and staff member comes from making a key shift in collective thinking. If educators view themselves as running on a treadmill, exerting effort but failing to make forward progress, then personal improvement feels impossible.

However, if the same educators can imagine their personal and professional development set along an upward trajectory, a trajectory that leads to new views of self and teaching and new areas of knowledge and expertise, then this commitment to learning can be the source of constant improvement and reflection. This conversation is truly about embracing that which is infinite about teaching. A school year is finite. A lesson plan is finite. But the inner journey of being a teacher and a learner is infinite. An individual's understanding of others is infinite. The potential that resides within ourselves and our students is infinite. In that truth is the sustaining energy of being an educator.

Whether you've used this chapter to take stock of your personal commitment to teaching or to consider the larger commitment of staff members at your school, you can move this discussion from theory into practice. Articulate your commitment, identify your obstacles, and set goals to change your reality for the better. When you and your colleagues make this effort to stay grounded in professional commitment, your job satisfaction can improve dramatically.

 [*See handout* **5.4** *on CD-ROM*]

NOW WHAT DO I DO?
MOVING IDEAS TO ACTION

One weakness I see in myself as a teacher:

One area my students would cite as an area of improvement for me:

One area my supervisors have identified as an area of growth for me:

Here is one *manageable* goal I'd like to set for myself:

Here are the obstacles preventing me from reaching this goal:

Here are some of my strengths that will help me overcome these obstacles:

These are the people I can enlist to support and encourage my goal:

One person who is already more knowledgeable or better at this than I am:

One person who will help me stay motivated and focused:

One person who might share a similar goal and could embark on a similar mission with me:

The first small action I will take toward this goal is:

Notes

1. Futernick, K. (2007). *A possible dream: Retaining California's teachers so all students learn.* Sacramento: California State University.

CHAPTER SIX: POSITIVE VALUES

Staff members experience alignment between personal values and professional practice. Staff members exhibit a deep commitment to the ideals of teaching.

One of my most challenging and rewarding efforts

as a teacher was to guide young readers through the process of learning how to read for meaning. It wasn't enough for students to flip pages at home at night, returning to class claiming they had read the assignment. Without an understanding, appreciation, and application of the ideas in the book, one couldn't claim to have read the story at all.

To truly understand a piece of literature, we worked as a group of learners to figure out the text on multiple levels. We started with the basics: characters, setting, plot, vocabulary, and language. Clearly we needed these foundations in order to do anything else with the text. Next we explored devices such as allusions, metaphors, and analogies in order to identify the intent of the author. At this point, we were just starting to have fun. Next we identified primary themes, using this definition of theme: *the insight about human life contained in a piece of art.* Now we were getting into it! This took our minds out of identifying a simple plot line and steered us toward connecting our own lives and experiences to the writing. My students and I experienced tremendous epiphanies as we moved from "What does this book mean?" to "What does this piece of literature teach me about myself and the world around me?"

The discoveries I witnessed in young readers as they mulled these questions were utterly inspiring. But at times, the idea that we were reading only in order to discover ourselves limited us. For example, if we read a piece and learned that we were greedy or vindictive, we wouldn't serve ourselves or our world very well if we simply patted ourselves on the back for figuring it out, neglecting to improve our own attitudes and behaviors. The insight would be far less useful if we stopped there.

That's why I always showed the class one last overhead or embarked on one final discussion. The exact language varied from one piece of literature to another, but the point was always the same:

The reason we have to discover ourselves is so that we are better able to serve others.

Identifying and instilling values in young learners is one of the great privileges of teaching. It informs how we operate in the classroom, how we act in the halls, and how we view the community at large. Taking a similar approach with educators allows us to improve the quality of our work and the sense of satisfaction it brings us.

This chapter helps you seek clarity about your own values and mission, and the values and mission of your workplace. When these ideals are in accord, they allow you to better fulfill your own goals as an educator and sustain your personal and professional energy. This discussion is divided into various traits or values as they apply to teaching. Reflecting on these individual values helps you define what matters to you most in your teaching.

questions

TO CONSIDER

○ **Do you feel a** strong correlation **between your personal values and those of your workplace?**

○ **Are you able to effectively reach your own** personal values and goals **within your work?**

○ **Do you share a** reasonable and achievable sense of responsibility **for the broad work of the school and its goals and limitations?**

○ **Do you actively seek a** balance **between your personal health and professional performance?**

What Do We Mean by Values?

Over time, most educators develop a repertoire of guidance tips to share with students. The advice we offer is founded on strong principles and lofty ideals such as caring, equality, social justice, integrity, honesty, responsibility, restraint, and personal health. We construct language and practices that help guide students toward attitudes and behaviors that reflect these values. The same principles underlie successful teaching.

In fact, many people are attracted to education as a profession because they see it as an opportunity to work in a setting that promotes positive values. As in many careers focused on social responsibility, educators feel positioned to fulfill the grandest of humanity's ideals. This is one of the reasons teaching is such a challenging and potentially rewarding line of work.

But because of this intense desire to contribute toward societal good, educators can also feel tremendous pressure from opposing forces: political trends, media influences, and competing demands from students, parents, administrators, and the larger community. Think of positive values as a compass that guides educators in their work; losing sight of professional values can make educators feel lost.

One of the greatest dangers to career satisfaction is the disconnect that occurs when an individual feels that her or his values are at odds with the values of the larger organization. It is almost impossible to attain job satisfaction in a divisive workplace. However, when personal values and organizational values are in alignment, teaching can be an intensely satisfying profession.

Exploring Your Personal Values

Values can reflect a variety of concerns or philosophies. Defining the word loosely, you might describe any number of things that you "value": a healthy balance between work life and home life, cultural tolerance, or even a sense of humor among colleagues. For the purposes of this discussion, we'll focus on two values that are especially relevant to education: integrity and responsibility.

Integrity

When we think of the word "values," many of our beliefs can be summed up under the heading of integrity. Just as Chapter 5 explored the commitment educators share toward learning and teaching, this chapter explores our definition of "right" and "wrong" in the field of education. To gauge your own experience of integrity in the workplace, ask yourself the following questions:

- Do you hold strong convictions about what it means to be a teacher?

- Do you feel that the demands placed on you at work are fair and reasonable?

- Do you stand up for yourself professionally?

- Do you give and receive candid feedback among colleagues and supervisors?

- Do you voice your own beliefs and values, even if they run counter to those of colleagues or your school?

Returning to the compass metaphor is helpful for understanding integrity. Just as a compass lets you know whether or not you are headed in the right direction, your internal sense of integrity acts as a warning when you're straying from your personal and professional ideals. Likewise, your compass reassures you when you are doing the right thing.

How Was *Your* Day at School?

One way a school reflects its values is in the way it says goodbye to staff members. Schools that value collegiality make time to recognize and celebrate these emotional moments.

Patrick Henry High School in Minneapolis, Minnesota, has had a long-standing tradition of holding a farewell breakfast for teachers leaving at the end of the school year. Whether a teacher is leaving to take another job, for family reasons, or has been "pink-slipped," their colleagues think it is important to have a moment together to say goodbye.

In the past, the breakfast was a catered affair. But as leadership turned over and pressures mounted at the school, the breakfast fell off the radar—that is, until some of the veteran staff members decided that this ritual was too important to give up. They have resumed the annual breakfast despite having no budget for it. They simply set up a microphone and bring potluck food to share. This event costs the school nothing.

Part celebration, part "roast," this gathering gives the entire faculty a chance to honor departing colleagues by joking, telling stories, and voicing gratitude. The people leaving also have a chance to thank their colleagues and say farewell. Most importantly, this event is an important chance for staff to come together, experience a positive sense of closure, and actively participate in their shared values.

Responsibility

A complex and personal term for educators, "responsibility" can be used to frame many of our attitudes toward our profession. We are responsible for our professional duties and classroom performance. We are responsible for the academic performance of our students. We are responsible to our colleagues in terms of offering support and guidance. We are responsible for taking on other roles in the school so that it functions effectively. Finally, we are responsible to ourselves for finding a professional balance in all of these roles that allows us to succeed without burning out. It is little wonder that the value of responsibility can feel like a heavy burden for many educators.

As you consider this portion of your professional value system, ask yourself the following questions:

- How responsible do you feel for the broad work of the school and for its problems and limitations?

- Do you feel responsible for the tenor and environment in your own classroom?

- What level of responsibility do you feel for the academic success of your students?

- How responsible do you feel toward your colleagues?

- Do you feel that your professional values about responsibility are similar to those of the larger school community?

Once you can articulate how *you* feel about responsibility, you can look around your work setting to see whether or not this value is consistently represented in your professional life. This is not simply about shedding responsibilities; instead, it is about determining what you perceive as a fair and reasonable amount of responsibility. Your reflections should be about the responsibilities you presently have, the ways in which you carry them out, and the ways you share them with others.

This line of inquiry requires you to give everything you have to offer to your school and your students while still retaining a sense of your own limitations. This is a delicate balance, since part of your thinking leans toward wanting to do as much as possible for as many people as possible, while another part is more measured and reserved. Leaning too far in either direction will cause problems.

Aligning Your Personal Values with School Values

As you seek to live out the goals you defined in earlier chapters, the intersection of your own values and those of your school becomes critical. At times the values of an organization are imposed by external circumstances. For example, mandated educational policies are going to have an effect on how the school carries out its mission. Therefore, some of the practices of the school might not agree with the personal values held by teachers and administrators.

When you are faced with a conflict between your values and the values of your workplace, you need to ask yourself two questions:

- What elements of my workplace can I personally affect and modify?

- What attitudes and behaviors can I modify to better allow my values to flourish in the workplace?

At the center of these questions is your ability to develop not only a sense of what is important to you, but also your ability to act on these principles in your professional life. The wider the divide between your own beliefs and that of your organization, the more likely you are to experience the kind of resentment and burnout that lead to serious job dissatisfaction.

At times you may feel that your own social, political, or religious beliefs might not be fully reflected by your school and community values. That doesn't mean that coming to work in the morning requires that you leave your personal values behind; rather, individuals and organizations should work together to align attitudes and behaviors so they become consistent with their shared values.

One of the key elements to integrity is your ability to state discordant viewpoints. If you are not able to do this, you are forced to repress the tension and stress that would have been released if you were able to speak freely. If this essential element is absent from your workplace, it is a worthy goal to work toward. Here are some suggestions for how to create positive, affirming relationships to allow you to act and speak with integrity:

- When your internal compass tells you that a work situation is unfair or "wrong," speak up early and often. Letting workplace tensions fester inevitably leads to unhealthy conditions. A diplomatic approach is always best, so seek tactful, solution-focused ways to voice your concerns.

- Assuming conflicts are going to happen and stresses will arise, make sure you work at building a strong foundation of collegiality during the good times—relationships that will be able to withstand the tense moments.

These are only a few approaches you can take to create an environment in which your values are aligned with those of your colleagues and school. For more information about communication, teamwork, and positive relationships, see Chapter 7.

 [*See handout* **6.1** *on CD-ROM*]

PERSONAL INVENTORY

The items below describe frequent themes that arise in Search Institute's staff development trainings with educators. Use these items to reflect on your own experience of values.

You *hold strong values:*

	STRONGLY DISAGREE	DISAGREE	NOT SURE	AGREE	STRONGLY AGREE
My personal values are aligned with the mission and values of my school.					
The core reasons I chose to become an educator are supported by my workplace environment and culture.					
My own beliefs and values are respected by my colleagues.					
I am given freedom to allow my own values to inform my instructional practices.					
School values are clearly stated and are reflected in policies and procedures.					

You *share values with colleagues:*

	STRONGLY DISAGREE	DISAGREE	NOT SURE	AGREE	STRONGLY AGREE
I compliment colleagues when I see them acting with integrity.					
My responsibilities reflect a fair and reasonable balance.					
I voice my own beliefs and values.					
I respect the values of my colleagues, even if they differ from my own.					

Promoting Positive Values at the Institutional Level

The best way to be sure the school's values align with staff values is to build relationships among colleagues and supervisors that allow for frank and open discussion of integrity and responsibility. Begin by collectively asking some of the same questions you asked yourself about your personal values:

- What are our convictions about what it means to be a teacher?

- Are the demands placed on our staff fair and reasonable?

- Do we give and receive candid feedback among colleagues and supervisors?

- How responsible do staff members feel for the work of the school and for its problems and limitations?

Before you discuss these issues, it is essential to build trust. This takes time, and trust is ultimately achieved through actions rather than words; however, you can start working on this by asking staff (perhaps even anonymously) to respond to these questions:

- Are staff members able to voice their own beliefs and values, even if they go against those of colleagues or school?

- Are staff members encouraged to give and receive candid feedback among colleagues and supervisors?

If staff members indicate doubt or apprehension in these areas, this may be a sign that your school suffers from a conflict in values. **Staff members who do not feel safe voicing their concerns will likely experience tremendous resentment and burnout.**

If you are in a position of leadership and are committed to communicating positive values in your school, take the time to foster a climate in which it is safe to voice concerns or contrary opinions. This sense of trust and collegiality is essential before an organization can address the problems that cause job dissatisfaction for staff members.

It is important to note that an effort to define values does not mean abandoning school policy in favor of philosophical discourse. On the contrary, underneath higher principles such as shared mission, common beliefs about students, and communal professional goals, your school also needs a shared set of behaviors and attitudes that guide how staff members treat one another, including everything from respect for each other's physical possessions to consideration of each other's mental well-being. Holding each other accountable not only for the ideals but also for the actions is what makes your school's values real instead of theoretical.

Once you lay the groundwork for discussions about responsibility and integrity, you can begin to address the inconsistencies or conflicts that staff members identify. As you make improvements, the following approaches can be especially fruitful:

- Use a mediator to facilitate difficult conversations. When two or more parties experience a conflict of values, this is a good way to diffuse the intensity of the conversation.

- Seek systemic solutions rather than the personal ones. If individuals' personal values are in conflict with something institutional, seek ways to remove conflicts that are long-term and systemic rather than leaving situations to case-by-case, short-term solutions.

Colleague of the Week

Chances are when a new student starts at your school, she is not only welcomed in an intentional manner, but she is given a full picture of what it means to be a student there. Behavioral expectations, school policies, and procedures will be clearly laid out. But her introduction will go beyond that, and another layer of enculturation will happen: students will share stories, mythologies, and insights about the school and its staff. Over time, a new student will garner a full understanding of what it means to be a student at the school.

What about a new staff member? How well does your school communicate, "This is what it means to be a teacher and a member of the adult community at this school"? Beyond explaining what forms to fill out to have copies made or to report attendance, how clearly does your school convey what it means to be a colleague in the shared work and beliefs of your school? Reading your school's mission and values in the employee handbook is helpful, but that's merely scratching the surface; a deeper understanding of workplace values comes through experience.

Your school probably has a "Teacher of the Year" award, or perhaps even a "Teacher of the Month" honor. Recognitions such as these reward excellence in instruction. But what would happen if your school started a "Colleague of the Week" award? In addition to the student-focused recognition for outstanding teaching, what would your school value and recognize about being a supportive, reliable coworker?

Values are something colleagues live out in daily interaction. Whether you are struggling to retain your newest staff members or working to prevent burnout in your veteran teachers, it is essential that your school's values come to life through action as well as words.

 *[See handout* **6.2** *on CD-ROM]*

INSTITUTIONAL INVENTORY

Use this checklist to identify the ways that your school is already experiencing positive values among staff.

	STRONGLY DISAGREE	DISAGREE	NOT SURE	AGREE	STRONGLY AGREE
Our work culture places a high value on responsibility and integrity.					
Our staff members avoid gossip.					
Our staff members collectively work toward a healthy work environment.					

continued

	STRONGLY DISAGREE	DISAGREE	NOT SURE	AGREE	STRONGLY AGREE
Staff members accept a fair share of responsibility for the values of the school.					
Staff members are willing to work extra when necessary, but do not make a habit of overextending themselves.					

 [*See handout* **6.3** *on CD-ROM*]

CHAPTER 6:
SHIFTING FROM RESENTMENT TO VALUES

Consider the following shifts as you work to build positive values in your workplace:

WORKPLACE RESENTMENT	UNIFIED VALUES
My views of how to effectively teach children are in conflict with the views of my colleagues.	I need to intentionally name and speak my own views and let them inform how I teach each day.
School policies and procedures are in direct conflict with how I view teaching.	I need to purposely work within the school systems to shape the values we share as educators.
My school asks too much of me and gives me too little.	I need to protect myself against becoming overextended and be mindful of my own capacities.
The social, human reasons I chose this profession are not valued by the school and its mission.	I need to introduce and participate in key conversations about values and mission with my colleagues.

 [*See handout* **6.4** *on CD-ROM*]

NOW WHAT DO I DO?
MOVING IDEAS TO ACTION

Although it may be useful to have written or stated values for your school, these values are more meaningful when they are manifest in the attitudes and behaviors of educators. Gather as a group to complete the following exercise:

1. Brainstorm a list of shared values that you believe your school holds.

2. How do you see these values manifested in the school?

3. What do you see happening in your school that runs counter to or is at odds with these shared values?

4. Identify one thing that needs to change for actions to be better aligned with the school's values. How will you make this change happen?

Has your school found a way to map or live out its values? Visit www.howwasyourdayatschool.org to post your success stories and read examples of ways other schools are addressing staff climate issues.

CHAPTER SEVEN:
SOCIAL COMPETENCIES

Staff members are flexible,
resilient, and communicative.
Coworkers value teamwork in
decision making and conflict
resolution.

Imagine a school staff as a group of hikers scaling a mountain together. Sometimes the grade is steep, other times more gradual. At times the winds blow and the temperatures plummet. Other times the sun shines and warmth radiates. The conditions are variable, and it's always an uphill effort.

Now think about your own journey and your interaction with the other hikers. You might carry someone else's pack for a bit if he is suffering. Perhaps you'll share your canteen of water if someone is thirsty. You hope that your colleagues will do the same for you.

Now stop for a moment and think about the things you *wouldn't* do. Would you secretly dump your heaviest gear into someone else's pack? Would you jump on someone's back and yell, "Speed up!" Of course you wouldn't. Dragging down your fellow hikers would be cruel, illogical, and selfish.

No matter how well things are going, teaching is always on an incline. It's simply challenging work. But like the satisfaction that comes with physical exertion, teaching can also be wonderfully fulfilling. Therefore, it's imperative that as fellow climbers we share the work and take care not to make anyone else's climb more difficult.

Ideally, the "we're in this together" attitude of a staff doesn't revolve around a negative image or attitude such as "we're going to suffer together" or "together we're going to survive." This chapter is about teamwork. It's about recognizing that even though the climb is difficult, collegiality and strong relationships are important keys to success.

questions
TO CONSIDER

○ **Do you approach teaching in a** collegial manner?

○ **Do you recognize your own areas for** growth and learning?

○ **What kind of** relationships **do you have with your colleagues?**

○ **Do you seek** active and meaningful resolutions **to conflict?**

Plays Well with Others

Social competencies describe the skills needed to interact effectively with others, to make difficult decisions and choices, and to cope with new situations. Our ability to interact with others and to make daily difficult decisions is crucial to enjoying this work. The following questions for reflection break down the qualities and traits we need to effectively interact with coworkers:

• Are you an empathetic listener?

• Do you avoid negative competition with your colleagues?

• Are you able to respond to stress with humor and patience?

These questions are empowering because they reveal active approaches you can take toward your colleagues. You don't have to wait for the school to initiate formal training or some other intervention.

This is about making sure your approach toward other staff members is as respectful as possible. To that end, it's perhaps more powerful to state these questions as declarative personal goals:

- I will listen to others empathetically.

- I will avoid negative competition with my colleagues.

- I will respond to stress with patience and humor.

By making these social competencies central to your own behavior, you can take control of difficult conditions or situations. You can make these traits concrete in your daily interactions with others. **Although you cannot control the attitudes or behaviors of other people, you can consistently decide to treat all of your colleagues with respect and patience.**

A tremendous amount of research revolves around the reasons why teachers leave the profession. A host of contributing factors exist, from student and parent issues to salary to class size. But inside all this research resides a fascinating truth: the quality of the relationships an adult has with other adults inside a school setting is one of, if not the most important, factors in a teacher's decision to stay in or leave a school or the profession at large.[1]

The next time you're in a faculty meeting, look around you. The people here play crucial roles in your satisfaction as an educator.

Contributing to a Team or Competing in Misery?

No matter how hard a staff works at collegiality, teaching can be a naturally competitive work environment. To begin with, teachers are regularly subjected to institutional scrutiny and other open forums of public and private judgment. We can count how many kids sign up for our classes, how many parent complaints we receive, or how often we are invited to attend our students' games, performances, or graduation receptions. If we're feeling petty, we can "keep score," comparing our stats to those of our colleagues. This endless bevy of comparisons can be both intoxicating and potentially damaging to educators.

Competition with your peers is not an inherently bad thing. In fact, a sense of competition can be a healthy motivating tool in your own development. But played out negatively, it can also be divisive and crippling to collegiality. Positive competition manifests itself in the following ways:

- Attention to and appreciation of the good work being done by colleagues

- Conversation about best practices

- An ongoing example of a desired outcome as a teacher

- A constant reminder not to be complacent and to remain a learner

- A general sense of appreciation for being surrounded by gifted educators

Cast in this light, our sense of competition with peers can be a wonderful element of our professional development. There's a wide gap, however, between working toward being "as good as I can be" rather than "better than my competitors." The latter approach implies that there are winners and losers.

The trouble comes when teachers feel as though they are pitted against each other, competing in misery rather than being inspired by the strengths of their colleagues. If your sense of competition has a paralyzing or saddening effect on your work, you need to change the way you interact with your colleagues.

For colleagues to have a thoughtful conversation about competition, it is helpful to first recognize each other's strengths and weaknesses. There are students, skills, and content areas that are going be handled more easily by some teachers than others. If you can celebrate and learn from each other's strengths, the weaknesses become nonthreatening opportunities to share with each other and grow professionally. Competition is valuable when it provides you with a sense of where you are strong and where you could improve.

Instead of experiencing competition as a source of jealousy, there is another positive and powerful opportunity for healthy comparison: We want to be as good as the teachers we loved when we were students. Look at your current coworkers as additional role models, similar to the teachers who inspired you to enter the profession in the first place. Rather than functioning as opponents, your colleagues can provide the inspiration to help you attain your personal best.

[*See handout* **7.1** *on CD-ROM*]

PERSONAL REFLECTION ON COMPETITION

1. Write a list of your immediate colleagues. Next to each name, cite one specific element of their teaching that you appreciate and could improve in your own practice.

2. Identify other colleagues whom you view as models for how you hope to be as a teacher. Cite specific elements of their teaching that you appreciate and could improve in your own practice.

3. Think of favorite teachers you had when you were a student. Cite specific reasons you enjoyed being in their classes and reflect on how those same traits affect your present practice.

Notice that none of the personal reflections above are phrased in competitive terms; rather, they seek to show that your colleagues and role models are not competitors, but people who can teach you the most about becoming the teacher you want to be.

Conflict Resolution with Colleagues

Educators need social competencies in all of their relationships: with students, with parents, with committee members and community leaders. However, tensions between colleagues tend to be the most taxing. Even a normal amount of collegial stress or infighting within a single year of teaching can be exhausting. Student-centered tension, by comparison, is much easier to deal with.

Consider this: what advice would you give to a student who came to you saddened or stressed because of a disagreement or an unhealthy relationship with a peer? Your advice would inevitably be to address the circumstances and participate in the difficult conversations that would offer resolution. Most of this coaching would fall under the guise of "I know it's hard, but it's part of handling situations maturely."

So what about us? Our interactions with colleagues inevitably include trying moments, moments of escalated pressure in our work. Most likely, these are the sorts of issues about which we say, "I just don't have the energy to deal with this." But we know that in the long run, unresolved tension and stress are a tremendous drain on our enthusiasm, our enjoyment of coming to work, and ultimately our potential longevity as a teacher. It is one thing to have a pile of papers on your desk; it's another thing entirely to have simmering tensions in your department or strained conversations between staff and supervisors. Considering the energy already required to interact with our students, it's little wonder that colleagues might practice avoidance or isolation instead of tackling such matters.

There's a piece of informal self-reflection you can do to measure the level of conflict you presently experience with your colleagues. Ask your friends or family to recall the people you mention most often when you make negative comments about your work. Is it parents? Students? Administration? Or a colleague? Perhaps as you look at your own relationships, this would be one indicator of who either feeds you or depletes you.

If this exercise reveals an epiphany about tension with a colleague, take steps toward reconciliation. If you recognize that you are not working well with someone, ask why that relationship is making your work and life more difficult. Follow up with efforts to address or eliminate those tensions.

A little self-reflection may also be illuminating. Charles Dickens wrote: "No one is useless in this world who lightens the burden of another." The reverse of this notion is "No one is fully useful who makes another's burden heavier." Consider your own behavior as well as the behaviors of others. Remember that if you're behaving in a way that makes a colleague's burden heavier, you are both less capable of doing your jobs well.

My relationships with fellow teachers and administrators have been largely positive. I mention this because even while working in a generally positive climate with a generally strong sense of collegiality, incidences of staff tension were still meaningful enough to cause me palpable job dissatisfaction. But it's also important to reiterate that on my darkest days, on the days when I was having trouble remembering why I decided to be a teacher, it was always another teacher who was there to support me.

Because our relationships with colleagues have such tremendous potential to sustain us in our work, it is essential to foster collegiality and positive conflict resolution. Healthy networks of communication make it much easier to address all other obstacles to job satisfaction.

[*See handout* **7.2** *on CD-ROM*]

PERSONAL INVENTORY

The items below describe frequent themes that arise in Search Institute's staff development trainings with educators. Use these items to reflect on your own experience of social competencies.

You *are treated with respect by colleagues:*

	STRONGLY DISAGREE	DISAGREE	NOT SURE	AGREE	STRONGLY AGREE
My colleagues are thoughtful listeners.					
My colleagues and I are able to work through conflicts peacefully with an emphasis on meaningful resolution.					
My viewpoints and experiences are respected.					
My colleagues and I avoid unhealthy competition.					
Even if I am in disagreement with others, I feel free to speak my opinions.					

You *treat colleagues with respect:*

	STRONGLY DISAGREE	DISAGREE	NOT SURE	AGREE	STRONGLY AGREE
When a colleague talks to me about a concern, I am a thoughtful listener.					
I am able to admit when I am wrong.					
I do not impose my own values and opinions on others.					
I purposefully note and recognize when a colleague does something well.					

Building Social Competencies at the Institutional Level

As Search Institute trainer Clay Roberts says, "You hire for attitude; you train for skills." What Roberts means is that our human, social skills are at least as important (if not more so) as any professional aptitude we might bring to the career. In fact, one could argue that social competencies revolve around a set of skills, attitudes, and behaviors that are very difficult to teach. But these skills can certainly be tended to, encouraged, and supported.

Roberts and other trainers often describe relationships in terms of rungs on a ladder. Participants in my trainings have found this metaphor useful in interpreting the different levels of relationships we have with our colleagues. The graphic below offers a simple visual to help you think about your own relationships.

 [*See handout* **7.3** *on CD-ROM*]

RELATIONSHIP LADDER

LEVEL 5

Friends at Work
These staff members are individuals with whom an individual can relate not only as a trusted colleague but also as a close, personal friend.

LEVEL 4

Sharing Work Life and Personal Life
These staff members are the close peers an individual selects for deeper levels of personal and professional assistance and conversation.

LEVEL 3

Coping, Venting, and Guidance
These staff members are the group of close peers individuals can turn to for specific advice and comfort.

LEVEL 2

Professionals in Relationships
Staff members are able to consult with one another about school issues and curriculum conversations. Staff members are available for conversations about student conduct and schoolwide issues.

LEVEL 1

Where Everyone Knows Your Name
All staff members know each other's names and roles, and can engage in simple conversation.

Exploring Level 1: Where Everyone Knows Your Name

All staff members should operate at Level 1. Knowing each other by name is the foundation for larger and more complex interactions. If this basic foundation of collegiality is absent, it's not likely that a staff will be able to tackle the heftier issues that will inevitably arise.

Building relationships at this level means creating a social norm in which staff members know and address each other. For the most part, this relies on an individual commitment to creating this most basic of social interactions. To assist in creating that norm, here are some suggestions:

- At fall workshops, purposely create events that provide a wide range of social interactions and encourage people to meet others. For example, have randomly assigned tables at lunches in order for staff to meet a variety of people in a social setting.

- Throughout the year, follow simple routines that allow for social interaction, such as serving treats in the staff lounge one day each week.

- Dedicate some portion of faculty meetings to informal time among staff to share personal announcements or interesting news.

At the core of this approach is the acknowledgment that collegiality has merit and importance. If staff relationships are treated as marginal, they will remain marginal. The only way to have a truly engaged staff environment is to commit time and effort to creating one.

Good relationships with other staff members, more so than almost any other factor, keep teachers fulfilled, sustained, and joyful in a school setting. If we acknowledge the importance of connecting with fellow educators, the least we can do is greet each other in the halls.

Exploring Level 2: Professionals in Relationships

The ability to discuss basic school concerns is especially critical at the team or department level. In fact, it should be a given that these smaller groups of educators can operate on *at least* this level. The environment of a small team is ideal for establishing the core relationships necessary to make sound educational decisions and receive daily support in the practice of teaching.

This level is the benchmark for a functional, working faculty. Without this level, little else in terms of collegiality can be accomplished. Here are some strategies for building relationships at this level:

- Within working meetings throughout the year, create consistent groups that allow the same staff members to interact repeatedly. Create groups that include representatives of diverse content areas, grade levels, experience, and any other potentially divisive barriers.

- Provide fodder for informal and formal conversation. For example, have a staff book or film of the month to spark conversations other than the "business of school."

Connections at this level are critical to the sense of communal mission and professional calling that exists among a school staff.

Exploring Level 3: Coping, Venting, and Guidance

Level 3 represents a transition within this framework because it's the first level where individuals choose the people they want to connect with. In other words, a staff and department operate on the first two levels as a default setting for a healthy work environment. However, at tier three, the selection of peers becomes more voluntary and personal. These are the educators whom individuals can use as a support and a sounding board. While personal, this type of relationship is usually limited to issues that naturally occur at work.

At a work climate training I conducted in Texas, a classroom teacher asked, "I know I'm supposed to focus on the positive and offer support to the other adults in my building, but does that mean I'm never supposed to vent or complain while I'm at work?" My response? Of course not!

Much of this book is focused on being positive, hopeful, and supportive toward our fellow teachers and administrators. This attitude is a key element to creating a fruitful dialogue about job satisfaction. However, that positive attitude does not eliminate our need to blow off steam once in a while. In fact, one of the absolutely essential pieces of having a healthy life within the school is having adults we *can* turn to in order to vent, pout, argue, and strategize. We cannot overcome our most challenging obstacles if we can't discuss those obstacles freely.

Looking at your own circle of colleagues in this level, it's important that you seek out people who not only let you blow off steam, but also help you seek solutions. Try to move conversations toward the question, "So now what are we going to *do* about this?" Doing so helps you benefit from venting without feeling trapped or overwhelmed by negative circumstances.

Although educators will select their trusted peers at this level, your school can make efforts to nurture these relationships:

- Set aside a time each week to recapture the useful conversations, observations, and plans of the previous week. Title it something like "Strategy Session" or "Objective Hour." Encourage peers to discuss the things that have been causing them stress that particular week.

- In the staff lounge, provide materials that encourage good conversation, such as "Question of the Day" cards. Include provocative questions about job challenges and coping strategies.

Exploring Level 4: Sharing Work Life and Personal Life

This is the level at which our personal lives and our work lives overlap. These relationships allow us to seek counsel about the pressure, challenges, and successes we experience both inside and outside the workplace. Our hobbies, families, and interests find residence in these relationships and help form a connection between our professional self and our personal identity.

By recognizing and valuing the personal side of educators' lives, your school can create norms that facilitate this level of relationship among staff members:

- Invite educators to announce and celebrate personal milestones during professional development time. Show that you value a balance between the professional side and the personal side of individuals.

- If possible, invite friends and family members to attend formal or informal staff celebrations.

It's true that these efforts extend beyond the minimum requirements of professional development; however, treating educators like whole people sends the message that you are genuinely committed to their long-term job satisfaction.

Exploring Level 5: Friends at Work

Level 5 relationships are the only professional relationships that overlap entirely with the principles of friendship. In fact, we might spend very little time talking about work with these colleagues. This does not necessarily mean that your social life should supersede the other functions of professional relationships; however, there is little doubt that in a job as potentially taxing as teaching, we all need trusted friends.

Workplaces cannot force such friendships to occur, but it is important to honor and accept this higher level of relationship as a source of support.

- Create welcoming staff lounges and other spaces where staff members can feel comfortable connecting personally as well as professionally.

- Schedule an unstructured social event that allows staff members to interact without guidelines or an agenda.

Too often "socializing" is seen as a waste of time. Viewed in a different light, friendships have the power to sustain educators and protect them from feeling isolated or hopeless.

Please note that even at these highest levels of relationship, staff members don't have to become best friends. The point of building social competencies across these levels is so that all educators are able to work well together in the service of each other and the students.

[*See handout* **7.4** *on CD-ROM*]

INSTITUTIONAL INVENTORY

Use this checklist to identify the ways that your school is fostering positive relationships among staff.

	STRONGLY DISAGREE	DISAGREE	NOT SURE	AGREE	STRONGLY AGREE
Our staff members have the time and space necessary to build positive relationships.					
Our school publicly recognizes good work by staff.					
The school provides unstructured social time for staff throughout the year.					
The school welcomes new staff in an intentional, relationship-building manner.					

Putting Social Competencies into Action

The value of a conversation about staff climate is perhaps best measured by its commitment to moving beyond conversation and toward action. Put bluntly, talk is cheap. Talk that results in improvements to the organization is truly worthwhile.

One opportunity for putting these ideas into practice is the hiring process. As you work to fill a position, you may conduct countless interviews of candidates. You will weigh and consider letters of recommendation, academic background, and responses to interview questions. But do you remember to stop and ask the question, "Would I want to work every day with this person? Does she ask good questions? Does she value teamwork? How will her interpersonal skills affect our current level of collegiality?"

While these considerations certainly do not trump someone's ability to teach and deliver content to students, it's absolutely critical to take these questions seriously. You are not simply hiring the students' teacher; you are hiring the staff members' coworker. If you fulfill the needs of both of these roles, you strengthen not only the individual teaching position, but the entire network of social competencies among your staff.

How Was *Your* Day at School?

We all know, logically, that we need to get along with our colleagues. We know it's a good idea to compliment others, and we appreciate recognition for our successes. We also know that strong relationships with colleagues are vital to our job satisfaction. But we're busy. We're tired. We're occupied with student concerns. We just don't have the time to dedicate to these efforts, or perhaps we lack a sense of *how* to actually create these relationships.

As you reflect on your experience within a "relationship ladder" in your school, let Reservoir High School in Fulton, Maryland, serve as an example:

- Everyone in the building contributes $10.00 to the Staff Wellness Committee at the beginning of the school year. Committee members use funds to send get-well cards and flowers for illness or death in the immediate family of staff members, to purchase baby and wedding gifts, and to plan staff social events. The committee surveys all staff in an effort to plan activities that appeal to everyone—both the single teachers and those who are married and have children.

- One year the staff circulated a notebook, passing it from one teacher to the next. Each teacher wrote something special about the teacher to whom he or she was giving the notebook.

- The principal often ends the year by putting each staff member's name on a sheet of paper.

Colleagues go around the room and write positive comments on each paper. On the last day of school, at checkout, the principal distributes these papers with all the comments so staff members can end the year on a positive note.

And these are just a few of the small, tangible examples of a school that consistently works to foster positive relationships among colleagues. The amount of time and money spent is minimal, but the impact is tremendous. This is about being intentional. This is about being thoughtful. This is just about being kind. What could you start doing differently tomorrow?

 [*See handout* **7.5** *on CD-ROM*]

CHAPTER 7:
SHIFTING FROM COMPETITION TO TEAMWORK

Consider the following shifts as you work to build social competencies in your workplace:

ADVERSARIAL APPROACH	COLLEGIAL PARTNERSHIP
In order to avoid tension, I refrain from having conflicts with colleagues about important issues.	Tensions with colleagues exact a substantial toll on my overall energy and enjoyment of work, so I need to actively seek peaceful and sustainable means of conflict resolution.
No one listens to my concerns, so I don't speak up.	I need to build core relationships with my colleagues so that I feel supported when I want to comment on important matters.
I don't reach out to others because I have enough issues of my own.	I need to share concerns with others so that all adults have a network of intentional collegiality around them.
I'm afraid of gossip among staff, so I remain isolated.	I am a member of a group of adults who are all dedicated to the same goals and mission and are actively supporting one another.

[*See handout* **7.6** *on CD-ROM*]

NOW WHAT DO I DO?
MOVING IDEAS TO ACTION

1. Ask three or four people from your family and friends to recall the negative comments you make about work.

- Whom do you most frequently mention when you make these comments?

- Are your complaints symptoms of larger problems? For example, are you having difficulty communicating one-on-one, or are you at odds over larger problems (instruction, communication, attitudes toward students or toward education itself)?

- How do you seek solutions that address the problem you've defined rather than the person?

2. Next ask your friends and family to recall your most positive comments about work.

- Whom do they identify as the colleagues who influence you positively? Tell these people! Tell them that they make your job better.

- How do you use this positive relationship to work on conflict resolution?

- How can you mutually encourage each other to reach goals and solve problems?

- How might you collaborate with this person to make the changes you want to see in your workplace?

Notes

1. Luekens, M. T., Lyster, D. M., & Fox, E. E. (2004). *Teacher attrition and mobility: Results from the teacher follow-up survey, 2000–01* (NCES 2004-301). Washington, D.C.: U. S. Government Printing Office.

CHAPTER EIGHT: POSITIVE IDENTITY

Staff members exhibit positive self-esteem, purpose in teaching, and a positive view of the future.

In every educator's life, there is a moment of clarity or momentum or inspiration in which he or she decides to embark on the journey of teaching. The moment comes in myriad ways, on different timelines. Often referred to as a "calling," this moment is The Decision to enter the profession. There are as many different stories behind this decision as there are teachers in the world.

Elementary school teachers may come to teaching for one set of reasons, while secondary teachers may come for others. Some teachers view their long-term commitment to the profession in one way, while other teachers carry a different set of expectations. But press "rewind" on each *individual,* and teachers can identify and share the moment they decided they wanted to become a teacher. As someone who has made The Decision, you share that moment with every teacher who has ever taught. That experience is a universal connection among educators.

From that moment on, of course, our paths can diverge wildly. We operate in different settings with different students, managing different workloads and teaching different content. But The Decision is our common denominator.

Positive identity refers to this sense of self and purpose that you experienced when you made The Decision. As you read on and explore your identity as an educator, try to reconnect with the passion that led you to this profession in the first place.

questions
TO CONSIDER

○ **Do you have a sense of** personal mission **in your teaching?**

○ **Are you** optimistic **about your school, your students, and the world they live in?**

○ **Do you** enjoy your time **with students and colleagues?**

○ **What does** being a teacher **mean to you? How does it** shape your identity?

○ **What gives you** hope for the future? **How do you survive this job?**

○ **How do individuals and administrations** work together **to systematize ideal conditions for teacher retention and job satisfaction?**

"The Decision" as a Grounding Force

Teachers come to The Decision by recognizing that they want to help young people learn and grow, and in so doing, could help the world. I have yet to meet an educator who hasn't shared this core belief—admittedly to different degrees, but the belief is at the center of all teachers. In a strangely ironic way, the modern-day challenges of teaching, what with mandated testing, lagging salaries, and intense public scrutiny, also serve as a somewhat perverse gauntlet that weeds out the faint of heart and the weak of spirit. This is not comfortable work. This is work that is in one way the greatest work in the world, and in other ways extremely difficult.

A high school science teacher at Southwest High School in Minneapolis once commented to me, "A bad day of teaching is one of the circles of hell." Anyone who has taught knows the truth in this notion. But a good day of teaching—a day when things go just right and you leave the building knowing that you're good at what you do and that your students are glad you're their teacher—those days must rank somewhere near the top of professional satisfaction.

It is on those good days when The Decision remains steadfast in our minds. When The Decision occurred, it was made with images of vibrancy and connectedness, not with frustration or complacency. At times it can feel like a long rope tied to both our own boat and the dock from whence we embarked. We can see it behind us, knowing that it secures us to the goals and principles we used to make the decision to enter the journey.

The Decision can be the reenergizing force we rely on when we step back from the daily realities of teaching and wonder if we chose correctly. "*Why* did I choose this life again?" The more accurately we can recall that answer and the more central that answer becomes to our coping skills, the better prepared we are for processing our rougher moments.

This idea of going backward into ourselves in order to move forward is all the more germane in today's educational arena—one in which present conditions do little to celebrate the powerful intentions of teachers and do a great deal of damage to the energies that sustain them. In some instances, it seems as though the challenges that educators face can lead them to lose sight of why they entered the profession to begin with.

Even more sadly, most teachers probably *do* remember why they chose the profession, but have encountered enough obstacles in their teaching that they are unable to perform their work in a way that remains true to their own intentions.

Revisiting our initial passion for teaching can be transformative in an educator's work life. Exploring personal identity allows us not only to reflect on past idealism, but also to plan for a meaningful future in education.

Playing to Your Strengths

"Let me introduce myself." This is probably the opening line to most school years. Sometimes teachers introduce themselves initially only by name, subject, class hour, and room number: "Mr. Blanski. Health.

Third hour. Room 315." But at some point, there's a moment when a teacher reveals his true "Self" to his students. A teacher's Self refers not to his daily mood or disposition, but to the identity that underlies his commitment to teaching.

In many ways, this definition of Self is analogous to the difference between "weather" and "climate." Weather is a daily experience, but climate refers to long-term, overall patterns. A single rainy day would not transform a desert into a rain forest. A cold day in summer would not mean that the climate has cooled. Weather is a temporary state, but climate is the more macro state of a larger global context.

Our Self operates in much the same way. Throughout this book, we've explored the notion that we can improve the larger patterns of our behavior—and, by extension, our identity. In this sense, Self-improvement does not mean changing our classroom reading assignments or the classes we teach. Those are more like changes in the weather. Instead, improving an educator's Self is a process of transforming, analyzing, and connecting with the permanent climate, which has vastly more influence over how we view our work.

One of the leading indicators of burnout in teachers is a depersonalization of the work itself. Teachers who burn out no longer identify themselves inside of their work—they feel neither invested in nor successful at reaching students and colleagues.[1] Letting our true Self emerge in the workplace allows us to connect to our work, colleagues, and students in a significantly stronger fashion than if we limit our Self to being an automaton who shows up to perform a repetitive task. In part, forming a strong sense of personal identity means validating your unique strengths. Students almost always make a distinction between the "smartest" teacher and the "best" teacher. This leaves educators with the difficult challenge of becoming one and the same. As you look around you at different "types" of teachers, several stock characters emerge, each with strengths and flaws. Read through this list and identify which type or types reflect your Self:

> **Content Master** Brilliant. Encyclopedic knowledge of subject matter. Lecturer. Commands through intellectual prowess.

> **Classroom Manager** Organized. Rules-oriented. Orderly. Systematic.

Entertainer Energetic. Humorous. "Kid-friendly." Dynamic.

Disciplinarian Strict. Rules by authority. Intimidating.

Of course, no single teacher is any one of those characters: we are all hybrids of each depending on the day, the situation, our own mood, the behavior of our students, and countless other wrinkles that can affect our performance and energy.

As you reflect on your own strengths and identity as an educator, how do your observations relate to your future? By looking back on the ideals that led you to teaching and by examining your present strengths, you can begin to more clearly see the hopeful future that awaits you.

Renewing Your Sense of Purpose

Aren't you glad you're a teacher? Aren't the stories you tell about your work inevitably dramatic, entertaining, even surreal to people who don't work in a school? Don't you sometimes marvel at the talents and abilities of your students and colleagues? Most importantly, do you often take time to think about these questions and celebrate your work?

It's noteworthy that the discussion about healthy teaching and healthy adults rests so squarely in the same values we hold for our students: gratitude, patience, humor, humility, and generosity are just a few of the hallmarks of the healthy teacher. Part of the focus on positive identity means an ability to be gracious toward ourselves and others.

Teaching is one of the few professions in which doing the best job possible actually creates additional work. The more we assign, the more we grade. The more ambitious our lesson plans, the more effort we'll have to make in order to get them done. Moving forward can often feel like moving backward.

That, of course, is why teachers are not only some of the most hardworking professionals, but also some of the most self-critical. We can counter this self-deprecating tendency by cultivating a strong sense of purpose. We should be able to wrap up each school day by congratulating ourselves on a successful day of teaching. It's too easy to focus on what you *didn't* get done or on what *didn't* go well. The long-term health of your career relies heavily on your ability to dismiss such negative thinking and to focus on your strengths and opportunities for improvement. Spend some time each day focusing on what you *did* get done and what *did* go well.

Articulating Individual Strengths

As a soccer coach, one of my primary goals for each season was to make sure that when the time came for the year-end banquet, I had something good to say about every player. It was easy to say things about the captains or the superstars on the team. But what about players whose gifts and talents weren't so readily apparent? Adding to the challenge, I tried to make sure my comments weren't really about soccer. I don't think parents or players came to the banquet just to hear me tell everyone how good they were at scoring goals. Instead, they wanted to hear something about their child—something unique about who they were as individuals.

My assistant coach Cookie and I worked hard from the first day of tryouts until the last day of the season to record positive traits about each player. When it came time to plan our banquet at the end of the season, we felt as though we could speak with authenticity and sincerity about each player—in such a way that even the parents would gain new insights about their children's strengths. While challenging, this was also the most fulfilling part of coaching. As you view your own work, try to apply the same thinking to yourself and to your colleagues. Imagine that you are planning a similar year-end staff banquet. How are you logging the great work of colleagues? How can you articulate the strengths of your peers? The difference between a school year and a soccer banquet is that with your colleagues, there's no need to store the good observations until a later date. Get in the habit of speaking the good things you are thinking. Say them to your peers. Say them to yourself. Few things are better at changing a staff's view of itself and its work than getting in the habit of observing, naming, and stating the positive things they do.

Don't forget to include yourself in this reflection. As you go through each day, think about positive observations you would make about your performance. You may not have had a day full of clear triumphs, but that doesn't mean you didn't have a successful day.

Moving toward Optimism

Frankly, the language and conversation used to describe teaching can be discouraging. "Long-range planning" is usually a phrase that means "fixing something that is wrong." We are more likely to have meetings about what is going wrong than celebrations of what is going right. Challenging students may get more attention than those who are doing well. Add it all up, and it's easy to see why optimism can sometimes be at a premium for educators. **The great challenge of modern education is that, for the most part, educators are being asked to solve problems they didn't create using strategies they didn't choose.** Therefore, pessimistic reports about youth are really pessimistic reports about schools.

This is why teachers must make a conscious decision to *choose optimism*. Whether you do this individually or collectively, make an intentional decision to focus on what's going well within a school and a community. If a staff doesn't announce its good work to itself, it might not get announced at all. If each individual doesn't make an effort to say thank you to colleagues, gratitude may not happen. Consider these questions:

- Does your school consistently and publicly recognize the good work being done by staff?

- Do you personally praise colleagues when you notice them doing something well?

- Do you acknowledge yourself when you've done a good job?

- Do your students and parents tell you when you've done a good job?

- Does your administration recognize your good work?

Deciding to focus on positive opportunities isn't a denial of the real challenges facing schools and educators. Those realities may or may not change. But we don't need to hear more about what's going wrong. We need to turn our attention to the small and large successes we're accomplishing.

Our positive identity is created out of a whole series of moments of success, weathering of hardships, and connections with others. We need to laugh when our students are funny. Marvel at their creations. Joke with colleagues. Share our struggles. Ask for help. Rejoice at successes. This rich tapestry of moments that make up the life of a teacher is the very thing that creates our identity—both as a teacher and as a human. That is, quite simply, the joy of teaching.

 [*See handout* **8.1** *on CD-ROM*]

PERSONAL INVENTORY

The items below describe frequent themes that arise in Search Institute's staff development trainings with educators. Use these items to reflect on your own experience of positive identity.

You *experience a positive teaching identity:*

	STRONGLY DISAGREE	DISAGREE	NOT SURE	AGREE	STRONGLY AGREE
I feel optimistic in my work.					
I feel despite whatever conditions might exist in my school, I can still be an effective educator in my classroom.					
I enjoy telling people I am a teacher.					
I feel I have adequate control over what happens to me at school.					
I have a realistic but hopeful view of my future as a teacher.					
I am optimistic about the role education can play in society at large.					

You *build positive identity in your fellow educators:*

	STRONGLY DISAGREE	DISAGREE	NOT SURE	AGREE	STRONGLY AGREE
I talk with my colleagues about our hopes for the future.					
I tell colleagues what I appreciate about them.					
I work with colleagues to focus on positive opportunities rather than negative complaints.					

How Was *Your* Day at School?

Sharon Ewing-Milne has been a teacher in Nova Scotia for 28 years. Teaching is her passion, and she has never considered another career for herself. She lives in the community where she teaches. She gets cards from former students who have chosen teaching as a career because of her influence. Sharon is a lifelong learner, always thrilled to discover along with her students. How has she stayed this committed for so long?

It's all about candles.

Sharon recalls preparing to speak at a retirement party for two colleagues who had taught for 30 years. As she was developing her speech, she came across the following quote:

> *"A good teacher is like a candle—it consumes itself to light the way for others."*

At the time, it seemed like a good quote and a powerful image. But Sharon has since thought further on what the quote really says. She now realizes that the notion of being consumed (or even extinguished) in order to serve others doesn't really sound appealing. Or healthy.

Sharon chooses to view her light differently now. She sees herself more like an oil lamp, one that can be refilled by students, colleagues, friends, and family members. Certainly there are times when her wick doesn't burn as brightly, or her oil is low. But she isn't being consumed. She simply needs to refill. Sharon says that if she were to rewrite the quote, it would sound like this:

"A good teacher is like an oil lamp. It consumes itself to light the way for others and fuels itself from the joy of those who have discovered where their journey leads."

And at the times when the wind really blows, and the flame is close to going out, Sharon's colleagues gather around her, protecting her flame and blocking the winds so she can continue to be a bright light for others.

Promoting Positive Identity at the Institutional Level

Earlier we used the word "climate" to refer to larger patterns of attitude and behavior. In the context of a whole school, climate means the work culture or the consistent experience of working in a particular setting. But just as the earth's climates are interconnected and complicated, a school's work climate is similarly linked to several spheres of identity or experience:

> A *global community* that places pressure on the educators and students.

> A *national culture* that creates laws, expectations, and mandates for educators.

> A *state culture* that sets funding, testing, and other external factors in place.

> A *community culture* that sets expectations, provides specific goals, and demands particular performance.

> A *district-wide culture* that creates policies, practices, and beliefs that directly affect your work.

> A *school culture* that is shared by staff, educators, and students.

> A *staff culture* that is distinct from the larger school climate.

> A *department or team culture* that most likely has the most direct effect on your enjoyment of your work.

> A *social culture* composed of colleagues with whom you might spend your free time.

Think of the many ways these spheres interact. A dysfunctional department might derail positive things happening at the staff level. A positive staff climate might mitigate some of the negative factors that are happening at the school level. Spending time with a negative peer group might very well erase some of the positive aspects you experience as a member of the larger school community. It's critical to pinpoint how our own dealings with these group identities personally affect us. Each individual needs to be mindful of how these spheres are interacting, and most importantly how the individual is interacting within them. The number of influences that affect your work is staggering. However, these external influences should not cause you and your colleagues to give up on the concept of positive identity. On the contrary, gaining perspective about these layers of influence can help you overcome the obstacles to defining a strong sense of purpose and meaning in your work.

The Power of Collective Identity

Let's return to our earlier discussion of an individual's Self. While each teacher is distinct, the collective body of a school staff possesses its own identity—a sort of School Self in its own right. A staff has a character, a shared sense of mission, a "feel," and an emotional continuum. This school identity can communicate a personality that is palpable to an outsider. Walk into ten separate schools—or ten different teachers' lounges—and you can discern quite readily what each school's collective identity is like. Do you sense tension? Joy? Laughter? Does it feel like a happy family or an awkward cocktail party?

The elements that make up this collective sense of Self are mysterious. Any situation in which a group of randomly chosen, bright, committed adults is lumped together into an intense setting promises to create a group identity that is entirely unique, challenging, and inherently complex. The challenge then is to create as much of a shared sense of Self as possible while protecting and encouraging individual personalities.

Essentially, in the same way that an individual teacher can say to a classroom, "Let me introduce myself," a school as a whole should be able to say to a new staff member, "Let us introduce our Self." The stronger this shared sense of Self becomes, the more resilient and mindful the entire staff experience will become.

Putting Positive Identity into Action

This book can help you change the conversations, attitudes, behaviors, and even policies directed at teachers. It's about making your job and life more fruitful and invigorating. It's about connecting you to your colleagues, students, communities, administrators, and profession in more powerful ways. It's about you connecting to your own values and personal missions more meaningfully. This is about you loving teaching more. And the end result? A school full of teachers who are more engaged in the education of students and the broad mission of creating healthy, happy, and successful children.

 [*See handout* **8.2** *on CD-ROM*]

INSTITUTIONAL INVENTORY

Use this checklist to identify the ways that your school is already building positive identity among staff.

	STRONGLY DISAGREE	DISAGREE	NOT SURE	AGREE	STRONGLY AGREE
Our school has a satisfying, sustainable work climate.					
Our school clearly values the contributions of staff members.					
Our school actively builds a sense of community among staff.					
Our school tends to the "staff climate" within the "school climate."					
The collective identity of our school is positive, collaborative, and welcoming.					

 *[See handout* **8.3** *on CD-ROM]*

CHAPTER 8:
SHIFTING FROM FUTILITY TO HOPE

Consider the following shifts as you work to build positive identity in your workplace:

FEELING STUCK AND HOPELESS	PLANNING FOR A POSITIVE, SUS-TAINABLE CAREER IN EDUCATION
I can no longer reach my students the way I used to.	I need to revisit the core values I held when I entered the profession and seek active ways to live out these values in the workplace.
I'm bored with teaching.	I need to seek new professional, social, and intellectual opportunities in order to sustain my interest.
No matter how hard I work, every year comes with the same challenges and disappointments.	I need to work continually to not only seek short-term solutions to challenges, but also create ongoing means of improvement.
I have no friends at work.	I need to seek out relationships that offer me happiness and camaraderie in the workplace.
Teaching has completely taken over my life.	Teaching is a balanced and rewarding piece of my larger sense of identity.

 [See handout **8.4** *on CD-ROM]*

NOW WHAT DO I DO?
MOVING IDEAS TO ACTION

Inside this circle, list the reason or reasons you became a teacher.

Outside the circle, list your strengths, abilities, talents, activities, and beliefs that ground you, sustain you, and keep you going in your profession.

Follow up on these influences that feed you as an educator. Because these are the things that sustain you, take action to increase these experiences:

- If you feel supported by another person, tell that person how valuable her or his influence is. Take more time to spend with that person.

- If you are energized or inspired by an activity, commit to the activity and make time for it.

- If you feel compelled by a philosophy or a set of beliefs, read, study, and contemplate this belief system further.

Notes

1. Byrne, B. M. (1999). The nomological network of teacher burnout: A literature review and empirically validated model. In R. Vandenberghe & A. M. Huberman (Eds.), *Understanding and preventing teacher burnout: A sourcebook of international research and practice* (p. 55). Cambridge: Cambridge University Press.

Epilogue:
Before the Bell Rings

I have never been much of a planner. Entering into the classroom (or the semester), I usually have a starting point in mind and an ending point somewhere "out there." That means that on any given lesson, students and I travel through a series of tangents in our discussions, some more related than others. But glancing at the clock at the end of each hour, knowing I have only two or three minutes left before the bell rings, I always make a final attempt to encapsulate the past 45 minutes into a kernel of truth or reason. This has always been one of my favorite challenges of teaching. As I come to the end of this book, I feel a similar desire to make sure you're walking out the proverbial classroom door with the best possible sendoff.

I feel more excited and energized than ever about the profession of teaching. As I've taken the ideas, research, imagery, and advice of this book for a two-year test drive, I've met with small groups of teachers struggling with the challenges of urban education. I've done keynote addresses to halls full of educators. I've led faculty meetings. I've led trainings for administrators. While these are rich experiences in and of themselves, what is even more inspiring is the updates I get from individuals and schools who have begun rethinking what it means to be healthy, happy, and balanced in the work of teaching. Comments such as, "It feels different now," or, "Things are starting to change," give me endless hope that we *are* in control of our future.

So, like any ambitious teacher, I also feel compelled to give you some homework. The end of this book is only a starting point.

The ending point, a point that resides somewhere beyond where you might presently see, is a future in which you experience a happier and healthier workplace. Your homework is to take on the challenges, discomfort, and hard thinking that will make this theoretical workplace a reality.

Along the way, share your story with others. Work together on the changes you want to see. Publicize your goals and accomplishments. Process your difficulties and challenges. But never stop moving forward. Remember that we are all fellow students, learning that we can serve others while still maintaining our own satisfaction with our work, life, family, and health.

To share your story and read about what others are doing to improve their job satisfaction, visit www.howwasyourdayatschool.org. Learn about book quantity discounts and training packages to help your school make broader efforts.

Acknowledgments

Thank you to . . .

My students, who taught me all I know about teaching and have made me a better human being.

My own teachers at St. Anthony Park Elementary, Murray Junior High School, Minnehaha Academy, and St. Olaf College, who inspired me to join them in this work and gave me the models I use every day in my own life and teaching.

All of the teachers I've worked with, who are the unnamed coauthors of this book and the sources of the joy, laughter, and inspiration that fed my days of teaching.

The Curtis L. Carlson Family Foundation, for understanding that helping teachers *does* help students.

All of my colleagues at Search Institute, whose support of me and this work are daily reminders of the power and pleasure of working with adults who care for a common mission.

The Bulldog, N.E., for being the site of some of my productivity and much of my pleasure in writing this book.

My family and friends, who have always understood the challenges and joys of teaching and have been constant sources of support and love in my own life—especially my parents Kent and Katherine.

My editor, Tenessa Gemelke, whose strong hand, keen mind, and good humor guided me through the journey of writing this book and created a finished piece that is so much more than I could have envisioned.

My sons, Sam and Pete, who are my favorite students and greatest teachers.

My wife, Erika, whose love and support keep me grounded, balanced, and joyful. No matter what happens during any day of work, it's a good day as long as it ends with you.

40 DEVELOPMENTAL ASSETS
FOR ADOLESCENTS (AGES 12–18)

Search Institute has identified the following building blocks of healthy development that help young people grow up healthy, caring, and responsible. If you would like to learn more about the work Search Institute does with students, please visit our Web site at www.search-institute.org.

EXTERNAL ASSETS

Support

1. *Family Support* • Family life provides high levels of love and support.
2. *Positive Family Communication* • Young person and her or his parent(s) communicate positively, and young person is willing to seek advice and counsel from parents.
3. *Other Adult Relationships* • Young person receives support from three or more nonparent adults.
4. *Caring Neighborhood* • Young person experiences caring neighbors.
5. *Caring School Climate* • School provides a caring, encouraging environment.
6. *Parent Involvement in Schooling* • Parent(s) are actively involved in helping young person succeed in school.

Empowerment

7. *Community Values Youth* • Young person perceives that adults in the community value youth.
8. *Youth as Resources* • Young people are given useful roles in the community.
9. *Service to Others* • Young person serves in the community one hour or more per week.
10. *Safety* • Young person feels safe at home, at school, and in the neighborhood.

Boundaries and Expectations

11. *Family Boundaries* • Family has clear rules and consequences and monitors the young person's whereabouts.

12. *School Boundaries* • School provides clear rules and consequences.

13. *Neighborhood Boundaries* • Neighbors take responsibility for monitoring young people's behavior.

14. *Adult Role Models* • Parent(s) and other adults model positive, responsible behavior.

15. *Positive Peer Influence* • Young person's best friends model responsible behavior.

16. *High Expectations* • Both parent(s) and teachers encourage the young person to do well.

Constructive Use of Time

17. *Creative Activities* • Young person spends three or more hours per week in lessons or practice in music, theater, or other arts.

18. *Youth Programs* • Young person spends three or more hours per week in sports, clubs, or organizations at school and/or in the community.

19. *Religious Community* • Young person spends one or more hours per week in activities in a religious institution.

20. *Time at Home* • Young person is out with friends "with nothing special to do" two or fewer nights per week.

INTERNAL ASSETS

Commitment to Learning

21. *Achievement Motivation* • Young person is motivated to do well in school.

22. *School Engagement* • Young person is actively engaged in learning.

23. *Homework* • Young person reports doing at least one hour of homework every school day.

24. *Bonding to School* • Young person cares about her or his school.

25. *Reading for Pleasure* • Young person reads for pleasure three or more hours per week.

Positive Values

26. *Caring* • Young person places high value on helping other people.

27. *Equality and Social Justice* • Young person places high value on promoting equality and reducing hunger and poverty.

28. *Integrity* • Young person acts on convictions and stands up for her or his beliefs.

29. *Honesty* • Young person "tells the truth even when it is not easy."

30. *Responsibility* • Young person accepts and takes personal responsibility.

31. *Restraint* • Young person believes it is important not to be sexually active or to use alcohol or other drugs.

Social Competencies

32. *Planning and Decision Making* • Young person knows how to plan ahead and make choices.

33. *Interpersonal Competence* • Young person has empathy, sensitivity, and friendship skills.

34. *Cultural Competence* • Young person has knowledge of and comfort with people of different cultural/racial/ethnic backgrounds.

35. *Resistance Skills* • Young person can resist negative peer pressure and dangerous situations.

36. *Peaceful Conflict Resolution* • Young person seeks to resolve conflict nonviolently.

Positive Identity

37. *Personal Power* • Young person feels he or she has control over "things that happen to me."

38. *Self-Esteem* • Young person reports having a high self-esteem.

39. *Sense of Purpose* • Young person reports that "my life has a purpose."

40. *Positive View of Personal Future* • Young person is optimistic about her or his personal future.

The 40 Developmental Assets® for Adolescents may be reproduced for educational, noncommercial uses only. Copyright © 1997 Search Institute®, Minneapolis, MN; 800-888-7828; www.search-institute.org. All rights reserved.

Index

About the Author

Nathan Eklund, M.Ed., is a professional speaker and an educational trainer with 12 years of experience as a high school teacher. He lives with his wife and two sons in Minneapolis, Minnesota.

About Search Institute Press

Search Institute Press is a division of Search Institute, a nonprofit organization that offers leadership, knowledge, and resources to promote positive youth development. Our mission at Search Institute Press is to provide practical resources to help create a world in which all young people thrive. Our products are embedded in research, and the 40 Developmental Assets—qualities, experiences, and relationships youth need to succeed—are a central focus of our resources.

Additional Resources from Search Institute

TRAINING AND SPEAKING

Great Places to Teach

What can schools do to increase teachers' job satisfaction and retention?

Partner with Search Institute to ensure that educators in your school experience the same strength-based, asset-building school climate that you strive to provide for your students.
This groundbreaking professional development model:

- Delivers a positive and practical presentation with great real-life examples;

- Identifies the issues educators rarely have a chance to discuss;

- Provides ways teachers can support each other and improve workplace conditions; and

- Uses an open discussion format beneficial to new and experienced educators alike.

Available as a 30–90 minute presentation, a whole-day workshop, or in consultation modules.

Trainer Nathan Eklund strives to empower teachers and support their commitment to teaching. He is passionate about increasing educators' sense of efficacy and enhancing their relationships among their colleagues and with their students. He helps schools understand and harness the connections between work climate, teacher retention, and academic achievement.

SURVEYS

Creating a Great Place to Learn

Take a look at your school's learning and work climate . . .

Research tells us that a positive school learning and work climate is critical for student academic achievement and staff effectiveness. The *Creating a Great Place to Learn* surveys, one for students and one for staff, measure perceptions of a school's climate. The survey focuses on school climate within three categories: Relationships, Organizational Attributes, and Personal Development. Secondary schools can use survey information to identify areas for improvement and foster a positive learning environment for staff and students. Staff and student surveys may be purchased separately.

Benefits:

- Reports the perceptions of your school's learning climate through the eyes of your students and staff;

- Helps focus energy and financial resources to strengthen your learning and work climates;

- Encourages the establishment of a planning process that will lead to improvement in your learning and work climate; and

- Promotes the improvement of your school's learning climate using asset-building approaches.

The *Creating a Great Place to Learn* survey is appropriate for youth in grades 6 to 12 and adult school staff.

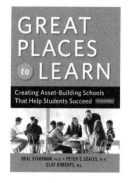

Great Places to Learn: Creating Asset-Building Schools That Help Students Succeed

Rooted in research on more than 2 million children, this foundational book is a powerful, positive guide to infusing Developmental Assets into any school community. From building awareness to sustaining system-wide changes, *Great Places to Learn* offers a step-by-step outline to guide school administrators, principals, and teachers through the process of integrating assets into their school.

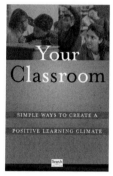

Your Classroom: Simple Ways to Create a Positive Learning Climate

Looking for a simple tool to share the asset message with teachers? This booklet introduces the Developmental Assets to teachers and then encourages them to foster all eight asset categories in their students through day-to-day classroom interactions. It's loaded with easy ways for teachers to build assets through tips on creating a positive classroom environment, building relationships with young people, and infusing assets into their existing practices. Sold in packs of 20 so every teacher in your school can have one handy.

A Quick-Start Guide to Building Assets in Your School: Moving from Incidental to Intentional

On top of budget cuts, changing curricula requirements, and dwindling instructional time, teachers and educational assistants are still expected to "do more with less." *A Quick-Start Guide to Building Assets in Your School* helps education professionals do just that: have more positive impact on students with less effort. Perfect for personal reflection or for implementing schoolwide strategies to get parents, students, and other school staff involved in creating healthy, caring classrooms.

Connecting in Your Classroom: 18 Teachers Tell How They Foster the Relationships That Lead to Student Success

If you want to be remembered as the best teacher they ever had, it takes more than knowing your subject and teaching it well. The teachers who excel, the ones who are remembered and whose students come back to visit them year after year, also make strong, empowering connections with their students. Eighteen teachers from across the country share their secrets to encouraging responsibility, empathy, and hard work—qualities that lead to academic and personal achievement—in their everyday interactions with students.

Powerful Teaching: Developmental Assets in Curriculum and Instruction

This resource shows education professionals how to infuse the assets into their existing curriculum and instruction without starting a new program. The book highlights research-based instructional strategies that teachers can use and adapt to their particular needs, plus real examples in Language Arts, Social Studies, Mathematics, Science, Health Education, and Visual Arts. *Powerful Teaching* allows teachers to focus on individual needs and foster the academic, social, and emotional growth of the whole student.

Pass It On at School! Activity Handouts for Creating Caring Schools

Schools where students feel valued, supported, and cared for are the best places to learn. This activity-based resource equips everyone in the school community—teachers, students, administrators, cafeteria workers, parents, custodial staff, coaches, bus drivers, and others—with ready-to-use tip sheets and handouts to create change for the better by building Developmental Assets. The handouts are grouped by where opportunities for asset-building can take place—in the classroom, cafeteria, locker room, nurse's office, in meetings, and more! It includes adaptable asset-building tips and ideas, engaging activities, and ideas for integrating Developmental Assets into your everyday efforts.